enjoy
of the Book of John

Best wishes

Go to Nineveh

Go to Nineveh

*Medieval Jewish Commentaries
on the Book of Jonah*

Translated and Explained

STEVEN BOB

PICKWICK *Publications* · Eugene, Oregon

GO TO NINEVEH
Medieval Jewish Commentaries on the Book of Jonah,
Translated and Explained

Pickwick Publications
An Imprint of Wipf and Stock Publishers
199 W. 8th Ave., Suite 3
Eugene, OR 97401

www.wipfandstock.com

ISBN 13: 978-1-62032-666-4

Cataloguing-in-Publication data:

Bob, Steven.

    Go to Nineveh : medieval Jewish commentaries on the book of Jonah, translated and explained / Steven Bob.

    xii + 160 pp. ; 23 cm.

    ISBN 13: 978-1-62032-666-4

    1. Bible—Jonah—Commentaries. 2. Rashi, 1040–1105. 3. Ibn Ezra, Abraham ben Meïr, 1092–1167. 4. Kimchi, David, 1160?–1235? 5. Malbim, Meir Loeb ben Jehiel Michael, 1809–1879. I. Title.

BS1605.52 B51 2013

Manufactured in the U.S.A.

I dedicate this book to my grandchildren,
Natalie, Ethan, Julia, and Naama

Contents

Foreword   *ix*

Acknowledgments   *xi*

Introduction   1

1   Rashi   7

2   Abraham Ibn Erza   17

3   David Kimchi   41

4   Isaac Abarbanel   66

5   Malbim   111

6   Divrei Simcha   137

Foreword

THE PAST SEVERAL YEARS have seen increased interest on the part of biblical scholars, theologians, and many clergy and lay readers of Scripture in the history of biblical interpretation. As more people have come to recognize the necessary but complex role that interpretation plays in discovering the contemporary meaning of Scripture, it has been natural for those interested in Scripture's enduring significance to look back in history to see how those who shaped our religious traditions reflected on biblical texts in light of their own times. In view of this healthy concern to understand and appreciate how Scripture was interpreted in the past, many readers will gladly welcome the present volume, which offers the first-ever complete English translations of five major Medieval Jewish commentaries on the book of Jonah.

These translations and the accompanying notes were produced by Rabbi Steven Bob, who has for many years served as the senior Rabbi at Congregation Etz Chaim in Lombard, Illinois. Rabbi Bob's work arose out of the context of adult education in the Jewish setting, and in their published form they will be of great benefit to many readers in that setting. In the past, Jewish readers who were not able to enjoy these commentaries in the original Hebrew did not have easy access to the insights they offer. Now, both individual learners and synagogue study groups can delve into the text of Jonah guided by these classical Jewish commentaries presented in clear English translations with explanations and theological reflections. In particular, the translations in this volume open up wide paths of learning for groups that study Jonah as the Haftarah reading for Yom Kippur afternoon. The availability of the great commentaries of Rashi, Abraham Ibn Ezra, David Kimchi, Isaac Abarbanel, and the Malbim on Jonah, a book that is so richly entertaining and at the same time deeply poignant, will be a great blessing to Jewish readers who seek to understand the religious message of Jonah for today.

These medieval Jewish commentaries are also important for Christian readers of Scripture. First of all, the interpreters in this volume offer perspectives on the book of Jonah that are different from the readings normally found in Christian commentaries. Even though many individual comments go their own way beyond the straightforward sense of the text, careful attention to the overall trajectory of each commentary will reveal a reading of the book that is both particular to that commentator's world and also genuinely engaged with the book of Jonah. For Christian readers to interact with these different engagements with Jonah is enriching. Second, Christian readers will benefit from what the commentators in this book have to teach us about medieval Jewish thought and the experiences of Jews in the Middle Ages. The significance of Jewish scholars in this era commenting on Jonah within Christian and Muslim cultural contexts is obvious. Third, the style of exegesis exhibited by these medieval Jewish interpreters greatly impacted Christian exegesis. For example, figures such as Nicolas de Lyra, Martin Bucer, Robert Wakefield, John Calvin, Richard Simon, and many others benefited from direct contact with the commentaries of Rashi, Ibn Ezra, and David Kimchi. The Jewish commentators helped pave the way for exegesis that was historically-oriented and contextual and at the same time explicitly religious. For these reasons and others, it is highly valuable for Christians to listen in on how these classic Jewish commentaries address this biblical book, Jonah, which is sacred literature for both Jews and Christians.

I am delighted to commend to all readers this significant contribution to religious education. Rabbi Bob's approach to translating and explaining these medieval commentaries is creative and illuminating. The notes bring out important aspects of the book noticed by the commentators, including the humanness of the prophet, God's mercy and justice, the nature of miracles, and the relationship of the God of Israel with the whole world. I want to express my gratitude to Rabbi Bob for making available in advance portions of this translation to our students at Wheaton College (IL), where Rabbi Bob and I team-teach a course on Judaism.

Michael Graves,
Armerding Chair of Biblical Studies and
Associate Professor of Old Testament
Wheaton College, IL

Acknowledgments

MANY PEOPLE HAVE ASSISTED me in the journey toward the completion of this book. I appreciate their encouragement, support and specific suggestions.

Professor Michael Signer of Notre Dame deepened my interest in the medieval bible commentaries through his own work. He generously read the early chapters of this project. He was a key supporter of this project until his untimely death.

Professor Michael Graves of Wheaton College encouraged me and helped through the final stages of this project. He read sections of this work and wrote the forward.

My good friends Rabbi Norman Cohen and Rabbi Michael Weinberg, each read a portion of my manuscript and provided ongoing support through years of friendship

The leaders and members of Congregation Etz Chaim provide me with a month long study leave every January. They understand that in order to continue to teach new and engaging texts, I must also continue to learn.

The participants in my Shabbat morning Torah study group patiently listen to my numerous references to Jonah.

Michele Miller proofread major sections of this book, saving me from errors. I am grateful to the staff of Pickwick Publication for seeing the value in this project and supporting its publication. My editor, Dr. Robin Parry's insightful guidance improved the quality and clarity of the text.

The teens of the Chalutzim program at Olin Sang Ruby Union Institute who have been part of my Jonah and the Meaning of Life class over years sharpened my thinking with their questions and comments.

My teachers at the Hebrew Union College, especially Haya Gavish, Avraham Alki, Dr. Michael Cook and Dr. Michael Meyer, introduced me to realms of Jewish knowledge and challenged me to work and learn on a higher level.

Acknowledgments

As I approach the 50th anniversary of my Bar Mitzvah I appreciate in a more profound way the Jewish foundation I received at Adath Jeshurun Congregation and at the Talmud Torah of Minneapolis.

The late Motke Yehezkeli of Kibbutz Rosh Hanikra, while serving as the Habonim Shaliach in Chicago, helped me see myself as a teacher while I was still quite young.

My HUC classmates helped me study during our years at HUC and have remained my friends for over forty years. For over thirty years, my study buddies and I have spent Tuesday mornings together studying rabbinic texts and solving the problems of the Jewish people.

My parents, Shirley and Fred Bob, filled our home with books and a love of Jewish living. They brought us rather than sending us to the synagogue. As a result my brother, Ken, my sister, Ellen, and I have devoted our lives to saving the Jewish people, each in our own way.

My wife, Tammie, has been my partner in all things. Her comments and suggestions keep me balanced.

I am proud of my children Lisa and Jason, Abby and Asaf, and Gideon and Molly. They each contribute to the future of their communities and to the strength of our family.

Introduction

THE UNIQUE PURPOSE OF THIS BOOK

THIS BOOK PRESENTS FOR the first time the full text of the commentaries of Rashi, Abraham Ibn Ezra, David Kimchi, Isaac Abarbanel, and the Malbim, translated into English with an explanation of these comments to make them accessible to the contemporary Western reader. I have also added my own contemporary commentary considering questions not raised by earlier commentators.

This volume does not present a verse of Jonah followed by all of the comments on that verse. Rather, it presents each commentary on its own, so you fully hear the voice of that commentator. The intention is that when you read Jonah with Isaac Abarbanel's commentary, you will understand and appreciate Abarbanel's reading of the text. As you move from verse to verse reading Rabbi Abraham Ibn Ezra's commentary, you will enter into his Jewish world. You will be able to imagine yourself sitting at a table with Rabbi Abraham studying the book of Jonah with him 800 years ago. I invite you to become a participant in the ongoing process of exploring the meaning of the words of the book of Jonah.

WHY THE BOOK OF JONAH?

I am drawn to Jonah because I feel that I know him. He is not a heroic knight of faith like Abraham. When God calls Abraham to offer his son Isaac as a sacrifice, Abraham gets up early in the morning and goes. When God calls Jonah, Jonah runs away. I know lots people who are like Jonah. I do not know anybody who is like Abraham.

I am also drawn to the book of Jonah because God gives Jonah a second chance. After God caused the fish to spew Jonah back on to dry land, God could have said to Jonah, "I forgive you for fleeing. Now go home. I will send another, more dependable prophet to Nineveh; perhaps Elijah is available for this mission." But God does not dismiss Jonah. God gives Jonah a new opportunity. This is deep forgiveness, forgiveness with renewed trust. God fully accepts Jonah's repentance. God sees Jonah as fit for the mission of carrying the Divine word to Nineveh.

We always want a second chance. We want a do over, a mulligan. We would like everybody we have wronged to give us a second chance. The question is, are we willing to give people who have wronged us a second chance? This does not mean that we simply forgive the people who wronged us. It means trusting them again in circumstances in which they had previously disappointed us. This is a serious challenge. Will we trust the person who mismanaged the money to again handle the finances? Will we trust the person who was less than loyal to again be our friend? The situations occur in each of our lives, at work, with our friends and our families. God's full forgiveness of Jonah should be a model for us.

Humor plays a key role in my life. This book contains exaggeration and humor including: the size of Nineveh, the extent of the repentance of the Ninevites, the animals of Nineveh putting on sack cloth, the storm and Jonah in the belly of the big fish. The humor of the telling of the tale draws us into the story.

WHY COMMENTARIES?

Traditionally, Jews read the biblical text with commentaries. This volume opens that world to a person whose Hebrew is not strong enough to handle the commentaries in Hebrew. Previous volumes provide quotes from the various commentators. Here the English reader can, for the first time, encounter the full text of the classic Jewish interpretations of the book of Jonah. By using this volume, you can enter a conversation with Rashi, Abraham Ibn Ezra, David Kimchi, Isaac Abarbanel, and the Malbim to explore the meaning of the book of Jonah. In doing this, you will gain a deeper understanding of Jonah and will also be introduced to the worlds and thoughts of the commentators.

Commentary connects the reader to the text, pointing out details the reader might have missed. Art museums often offer recorded commentaries for their special exhibits. You can decline the recorded commentary and walk around the exhibit just looking at the paintings and enjoying them. The commentary will draw your attention to aspects of the paintings you might have overlooked. The commentary might describe a new brush technique. The commentator could explain conventions that were well known in a particular culture. Once I learned from a recorded commentary in an art museum that, in Baroque painting, cherries represent fertility. As someone who is not an expert in Baroque art, I would not have understood this convention without the commentary.

Effective sports commentators bring you into the game. They explain what you would not otherwise understand. In a football game many things happen at once. The announcer will call your attention to the detail you might miss in the clutter. You watched the quarterback throw a long pass downfield to a receiver who then scored a touchdown. The commentator points out that the play was successful because of the block of the running back on the blitzing linebacker. He tells you that few running backs could have made that block.

We each read the biblical text through eyes conditioned by our experiences and knowledge. We cannot look at the text except from within the context of our lives. Likewise, the commentators write for the context of their time and place.

The commentators respond to problems in the original Hebrew text. The biblical text is bumpy. The commentator helps the reader overcome the rough spots, places where the text is unclear, including: unusual words, known words used in unusual ways, places where the referent of the image is uncertain, and problems with the narrative line of the story.

When we read a biblical book in translation we often do not see the problem in the text which challenged the commentator. The translator has smoothed out the text. The translator cannot present a text with "mistakes," even if those mistakes are in the original Hebrew.

I am told that when a Yiddish theater on the lower east side of New York presented Hamlet in Yiddish, the theater's marquee proclaimed, "Hamlet, translated and improved." When we read a biblical text in translation we should realize that the text is "translated and improved."

The commentators often quote a word or phrase from the verse that they believe requires clarification, in which case I present the word to be clarified in Hebrew in transliteration, generally followed by a literal translation. However, in certain places I do not translate a biblical word being explained because its literal meaning is unclear. The commentators seek to clarify what the word means. The commentators often quote from elsewhere in the Hebrew Bible without providing the source of the quote. I add these references in my explanations.

While the Christian commentaries on Jonah lie beyond the scope of this book, we should be aware that some of the comments recorded here are in response to the commentaries of Theodore of Mopsuestia, Jerome, and other early Christian writers. Writing in the fourth and fifth centuries, these church fathers authored polemics arguing for the superiority of Christianity over Judaism. They saw Jonah as representing the inferior nationalistic Judaism as opposed to the universal faith of Christianity.

They argue that Jonah refuses to go to Nineveh because he is angry that God expresses concerns for the non-Israelite Ninevites. They contend that as Jonah believed God should care only about Israelites, so Jews believe that God should only care about Jews. They contrast this particularistic position with their universal Christian image of God caring for all people.

The Jewish commentators do not refer directly to these polemics, but they all offer other more positive motivations for Jonah's flight. The medieval Jewish commentators lived at a time when Jews felt pressure to defend the validity of Judaism. Because we live in a more pluralistic post-polemic society, we do not expect the interpretations of Jonah to be a battleground for an interfaith debate. But by understanding the context that once existed, we will have greater insight into the commentators' efforts to put a positive spin on Jonah's flight.

The commentators use masculine pronouns to refer to God. As a translator I want to provide the text as they wrote it, not as I would have written it. So I maintain the masculine pronouns. I have used He, His, and Him with a capital "H" to refer to God. I use he, his, and him with a lower case "h" to refer to Jonah.

I present the commentaries of five giants of rabbinic biblical interpretation, Rashi, Abraham Ibn Ezra, David Kimchi, Isaac Abarbanel, and the Malbim. Each chapter includes a brief introduction, my translation, and explanation of the commentaries of these rabbis. The **words in bold** are my translation of their words. The words in standard typeface are my explanation of their comments. Some of their comments require little or no explanation. Other comments require a fuller explanation. The book presents the commentaries in chronological order. And often the later commentators respond to interpretations of the earlier commentators.

Following the traditional commentaries, I have included my own commentary on Jonah. After spending so many years admiring the work of these great scholars, I could not resist the temptation to "put on a uniform and get in the game." My Hebrew name is Simcha, which means joy. I call my commentary Divrei Simcha, which could be understood as "The Words of Steven Bob" or "Words of Joy." I hope that you find both translations to be accurate descriptions of the Divrei Simcha commentary.

1 Rashi

Introduction to Rashi's Jonah Commentary

RABBI SHLOMO YITZHAKI, (1040–1105), is better known by the acronym Rashi. He spent most of his life in Troyes, in the Champagne area of northern France. He studied in Worms in the Yeshiva, study hall, of Rabbi Yaakov ben Yakar and then in Mainz with Rabbi Yitzhak ben Yehudah. He returned to Troyes, where he established his own Yeshiva. Rashi wrote a commentary on the complete Tanach and on the entire Talmud. Either project would be considered a life's work. In addition to his scholarship, Rashi earned his living as a wine merchant.

Many of the stories which one hears about Rashi come, in truth, from old legends or contemporary novels. We do know that Rashi had three daughters who married scholars. His grandsons include the prominent scholars Jacob ben Meir, known as Rabbenu Tam, and Shmuel ben Meir, known as Rashbam.

Rashi's commentary to the Tanach provides the foundation for an ongoing conversation about the meaning of the biblical text. But as we shall see, later commentators feel free to disagree with Rashi over the meaning of the narrative of the biblical text. Jewish tradition can afford an open conversation about why Jonah fled.

Rashi's commentary on Jonah is much shorter than the later commentaries. He does not comment on each verse. His comments are brief. Rashi remains focused on the text. He does not launch into long theological arguments as later commentators do. Also, in general, Rashi's commentary to the prophets and the writings differs from his commentary to the Torah. Rashi's Torah commentary draws heavily from the Midrash. Much less Midrash existed on prophets and writings to which Rashi could turn.

In his commentary to Jonah, Rashi draws upon chapter ten of Pirke D'Rabbi Eliezer, a ninth-century collection of Midrash. Rashi explicitly mentions Pirke D'Rabbi Eliezer in his comments to verses 1:7 and 2:9. In other places he uses ideas mentioned in Pirke D'Rabbi Eliezer without stating his source. For example, in his comment to 1:5, Rashi expresses the idea that all the nations of the world were represented in the crew of the ship. This concept is found in chapter ten of Pirke D'Rabbi Eliezer, but Rashi does not include his source in his comment.

Rashi often refers to the Targum. Targum is the translation of the Bible into Aramaic, the everyday spoken language of the rabbinic period. By Rashi's time, most Jews did not speak Aramaic. The translation of the Hebrew text into Aramaic is helpful to Rashi in clarifying the meaning of difficult phrases. He shares with his readers how the author of the Targum understood the word. The Talmudic tradition attributes the authorship of the Targum to the books of the prophets to Jonathan ben Uzziel. It is therefore called Targum Yonaton.

Twice in his commentary to Jonah, in 1:6 and in 4:8, Rashi translates difficult words into Old French, the spoken language of his readers.

In his comment on 2:7, Rashi turns to other books of the Tanach, Second Kings 4:4 and Job 2:4, to present other uses of the word used in Jonah. In other cases Rashi uses words similar or related to the word used in Jonah. In his comment on 1:6 he uses Psalms 146:4 and Daniel 6:4 and in his comment on 2:8 he uses Lamentations 2:11.

Rashi's Commentary on the Book of Jonah

Chapter One

2. "*Ukara aleha, Proclaim upon it.*" The text here does not include what Jonah will proclaim to the Ninevites, it will be God's words, as is indicated in 3:2, **My proclamation.**

3. "*Livroach Tarshisha, To flee towards Tarshish.*" This refers to **the sea on which Tarshish is located; namely outside the land** of Israel. **He, Jonah, said "I will flee by the way of the sea because the Shechinah,** that aspect of God from which prophecy flows, **does not dwell outside the land** of Israel. **The Holy One of Blessing said to him, "By your life! I have agents like you whom I can send after you to retrieve you from there."**

An illustration of this principle can be seen in the story of **a ser-vant of a priest who ran away from his master and entered a cemetery,** where priests are prohibited from entering. **His master said to him, "I have servants like you whom I can send after you to retrieve you from there."** Rashi seems to agree with Jonah's belief that the Shechinah, and thus prophecy, is limited to the Land of Israel. And that therefore God does not call Jonah to prophesy while he is at sea. However, God's power does not end at the edge of the Land of Israel. God has other means, such as the storm and the fish, to retrieve Jonah.

What was it that Jonah apprehended that led him to conclude that **he did not want to go to Nineveh? He thought, "These idolaters are close to repenting, if I speak to them and they repent, I will have indicted the Israelites who hearken not to the words of the prophets."** God regularly sends prophets to the Israelites, calling upon them to turn from their evil ways and repent. The Israelites constantly ignore these prophets and con-tinue in their lives of sin. If the Ninevites respond to one visit from one prophet while the Israelites continue to ignore a whole series of prophets, the Israelites will be shown to be an inferior people.

"*Vayiten s'charah, He paid its fare.*" He paid in advance, while the usual custom of seafarers is to pay their individual fare upon disem-barkation. He not only advanced** his own fare **but paid the charter rate.** The possessive suffix on *s'charah* causes the phrase to mean Jonah paid "its fare." The text could have said that Jonah paid *hasachar*, the fare, or *s'charo*, his fare. Rashi concludes that the *ah* suffix indicates that Jonah paid for the whole boat not just one seat.

4. **"*Chishva l'hishaver, It thought it would break up.*"** A ship cannot "think" so we should not take the phrase "it thought it would break" literally but rather figuratively to mean **It seemed as if it would break** apart.

5. **"*Hamalachim, Salts.*"** In this context it means **the men who crew the ship.** The book of Ezekiel also uses *melachim* in this way.

"*Ish el elohav, Each man to his god.*" This phrasing, in the singular, shows that the sailors did not share a common god but that rather each sailor had a different god. In fact, **every nationality of idolater was repre-sented.** The ship then becomes a microcosm for the entire gentile world.

6. "*Rav hachoveil, The head of those who seize.*" We should understand it as **the captain of the crew who are sometimes called *chovlai hayam*,** those who take on the sea. **In the vernacular, Old French, Govirniyel.**

"*Mah l'cha nirdam, What is this to you O sleeping one?*" We should understand this unusual phrasing to mean **How can you be sleeping? This is no time to sleep!**

"*Yitashait, Will think.*" **This is language referring to "thought."** This Hitpa'ail verb occurs only this one time in the entire Bible. To understand it Rashi turns first to a related noun which shares the same three letter root, Eiyin, Shin, and Tav, found in another biblical verse. **It is like Psalms** 146:4 "*Ivdu eshtonotav,* **his thoughts perish.**" To support this understanding of this root, Rashi now turns to an Aramaic Pa'al verb with the same root, "***Malka ashit,* the king thought.**" Daniel 6:4. Based on these verses, Rashi concludes that our phrase means "God will think."

7. "*L'cho v'napilah goralot, Come let us cast lots.*" The sailors "cast lots" because they recognized that they were not facing a normal storm. **They saw the rest of the boats traveling peacefully on the sea, while theirs was breaking apart.** They conclude that this storm was a not a natural event rather a supernatural event caused by Divine anger at someone on the ship. **They said, "This is because of one of us!" We found this** comment in **Pirke D'Rabbi Eliezer.**

"*B'shelmi, In belonging to whom.*" This word is a contraction of three words, *b'ma'asav shel mi* which mean, "**In the acts of who**" among us.

8. "*Hagida-na lanu basher l'mi, "Please tell us in regard to whom* is this *evil upon us?*" The fact that the lot fell on Jonah convinces the sailors that he is the cause of the storm. Now they want to understand what sin Jonah has committed to bring about such a calamity. In the second part of this verse the sailors ask Jonah a series of questions about his life in order to learn the nature of his sin, which has brought the storm upon them. The verse begins with an unclear question. It means **against whom have you sinned that this evil should befall us?** Once the sailors know against whom Jonah has sinned they proceed with the questions to determine the nature of the sin.

"*Mah m'lactecha, What is your craft?*" **Perhaps you have sinned in your craft.**

"*Umai'ayin tavo, Where are you from?*" **Perhaps a decree has been issued against the people of that place,** and it accompanies you, **even though you are not there.**

"Vai-mizeh am ata, From what people are you?" Perhaps your people have sinned.

10. *"Mah zot asita, What is this that you did?"* **Why have you done this, to flee from such a ruler** as the powerful God of Israel**?**

13. *"Vayacht'ru ha'anashim, And the men tunneled."* The text uses this verb because the sailors, threw **themselves into the task** of rowing like **people digging a tunnel.**

14. *"B'nefesh haish hazeh, In this man's soul."* Rashi understands the Bet at the beginning of *"b'nefesh"* to mean "on account of." The sailors ask the God of Israel not to punish them *on account of* what they are about to do to Jonah. They say, We do not want to suffer **for the sin of our endangering his life with our own hands.**

16. *"Vayidru nedarim, And they vowed vows."* The text does not explicitly tell us the content of the vows of the sailors. They swore **that they would convert** to become worshippers of the One God of Israel.

Chapter Two

1. *"Dag gadol, Big fish."* Rashi seeks to reconcile an apparent grammatical conflict between verses one and two. In verse 1, the word for fish is in the masculine form, *Dag.* Verse 2 uses the feminine form for fish, *Dagah.* **It was a male** fish **and he could stand in an open space**, in the belly of the fish, **and so he was not moved to pray. The Holy One of Blessing intimated to the** male **fish and it spit him into the mouth of a female** fish**, which was full of embryos,** which pressed against the belly of the fish, decreasing the room available to Jonah. **There he was stressed and he prayed there, as it says,** in verse 2, *"Mimai hadagah, from the belly of the female fish."*

3. *"Mibeten Sheol shivati, From the belly of Sheol I cried out."* Jonah says that he called to God from Sheol yet he is not in Sheol but rather in the belly of the fish. Jonah feels **the belly of the fish is like Sheol to me.**

4. *"Kol mishbarecha v'galecha, All Your breakers and Your waves."* Why is the word "breakers" used here to describe the waves? **All the waves of the sea** are called breakers **because they break and divide the sea.**

5. *"V'ani amarti, And I said."* Clearly Jonah did not "say" these words as he was thrown into the sea rather he thought them. **When they threw me into the sea** I thought **I was dead** or about to die **and therefore driven from your sight.**

"Ach, therefore." The two phrases of this verse seem to be in opposition to each other and more appropriately connected by "but." Rashi explains how the word "therefore" connects the two phrases. Jonah thinks, *"'I was driven from your sight'* yet I **see** now **that you have kept me alive all these days** *therefore* **I know that *'I will again gaze at your Holy Temple.'"***

6. *"Suf chashuv l'roshi, Reeds were tangled about my head."* Rashi, following the Targum, understands the term *suf*, "reeds," in the text to refer to the "Sea of Reeds." Therefore Jonah says, **"The Sea of Reeds hangs from above my head."** The Holy One of Blessing showed him the Sea of Reeds **and how the Israelites crossed it.** Rashi now explains how Jonah could see from inside the belly of the fish. **The two eyes of the fish were like two windows and he looked out and saw all that was in the sea.**

7. *"L'kitzvei harim yaradti, To the bases of the mountains I descended."* **To the end,** the bottom, **of the height of mountains fixed in the depths of the sea did I descend.**

"Haaretz b'richeha va'adi, The earth, its bars against me forever." The text does not seem to express a complete image. It should be understood as, The earth, its bars **against me from above are closed, I will not** be able **to ascend forever.** The root of the word *va'adi* is Bet, Aiyin, Daled. Rashi draws our attention to a biblical example of the word *ba'ad* used with the word *sagar* to mean "closed after." *Vaadi* here in Jonah **is like** *ba'adaich* in **Second Kings** 4:4 "Go in and **shut the door, *ba'adaich*, after you,** and after your children." **So it is with every instance of *ba'ad* in the Bible. "Flesh *ba'ad*, after, flesh" in Job** 2:4 means **a limb after a limb.** Rashi argues that the use of *ba'ad* in our text is consistent with its use in other places in the Bible. He says it always implies completed action after or against someone. (In the Mikrot Gedolot edition of Rashi's commentary the Job reference is incorrectly given as chapter one)

"L'olam, Forever." The problem is if Jonah has already realized he will be saved, why does he describe his situation as lasting *forever?* **This is included in that which is written above,** in verse five, **"I said I was driven away"** so we should understand this phrase as, earlier **I said, "The land from which I fled is closed to me forever.** But now I know God will save me."

"V'taal mishachat chayai, You lifted my life up from the pit." The verb, *"v'taal,* you lifted," is in the past tense even though Jonah, at this point in the narrative, is still under the water in the belly of the big fish. Rashi explains that the use of the past tense is appropriate because Jonah had been deeper in the sea than he is by verse seven. **For I have already seen Gehenom and from there you lifted me up and now,** under water, **I am under your Temple in Jerusalem from where I said, "I will again look upon your Holy Temple"** and **"my prayers will reach your Holy Temple,"** as stated in verse 8.

8. *"B'hitateif, In the wrapping."* The image of Jonah's soul wrapping upon him is difficult to understand. Rashi, drawing upon the Targum's translation of this word into the Aramaic word, *b'ishtal'hayut* explains, **in a swoon and thus the soul is wrapped upon itself.** Our word is in a Hitpa'ail form, an example of this root, in a Niphal form, used to convey a similar meaning is found **in Lamentations 2:11, "The infant** and baby *bai'ateif,* **fainted."**

9. *"M'shamrim havlei shav, Zealously guarding utter futilities."* This phrase refers to the sailors as **they who worship idols.**

"Chasdam ya'azovu, They forsake their kindness." Rashi offers two very different explanations of *"chasdam."* **From the fear of God who is the source of kindness and goodness they,** the sailors, **have turned away but I,** Jonah, **am not like that. Rather with a voice of thanksgiving, I will bring offerings to you. This is according to Targum Jonathan. Pirke D'Rabbi Eliezer explains that the sailors abandoned their acts of kindness, which they performed to their idols and then converted** to the worship of the one God.

10. *"Yeshuata laYHVH, Salvation to The Eternal."* The text mentions a vow without explicitly providing the content of the vow. **My,** Jonah's, **vow is** to offer *shalamim* **and thanksgiving** sacrifices **for the sake of the salvation that is God's.** Rashi now turns his attention to the unusual spelling of *"yeshuata,* Salvation." Why is it not simply *yeshua*? **"Yeshuata is like *l'yeshuata.* This is similar to a phrase in Psalms 44:27 *"ezrata lanu,"* which is understood to have the meaning of *l'ezra shelanu,* to our help.** The extra letter Taf is in place of a Lamed at the beginning of the word.

Chapter Three

4. "*Nehpachat, Overturned.*" Jonah warns the people that Nineveh will be **destroyed. The text does not simply use the term destroyed because the term "*overturned*" can be used in two different ways, bad and good. If they do not repent then Nineveh will be "*overturned*". If they do repent, then that which was proclaimed concerning the people of Nineveh will be "*overturned.*" For they turned over from bad to good and repented.**

6. "*Adarto, His glory.*" From context we can understand that it refers to **his precious clothing** for in the last portion of the verse we read that the king puts on sackcloth.

7. "*Vayazeik, And he caused it to be cried.*" This is a Hifil verb expressing causation. The king did not himself cry out the proclamation to the Ninevites but rather he **commanded that it be publicly proclaimed.**

"*Hamelech ug'dolav, The King and his great ones.*" **By the counsel of the King and the nobles it has been commanded and proclaimed.**

8. *Vayikru el-Elohim b'hazakah, They cried out to God with might.*" "*B'hazakah*" could be understood to mean "mightily" but Rashi understands "with might" to mean exactly that. They used might to state their case to God. **They, the men of Nineveh, took hostage the mothers, separately, and the children, separately. They said before the Master of the Universe, "If you do not show us mercy, we will not show mercy to these** hostages."

9. "*Mi yodaiah, Who knows.*" Some readers understand God to be the subject of the sentence but Rashi understands the subject of the sentence to be the individual Ninevites who are sinners. **The one** who **has sins in his hand, shall repent.**

10. "*Vayinachem Haelohim, And God repented.*" The text uses the same word to describe God's change of heart as it does to describe the Ninevites' change of heart. In connection with the Ninevites' shift the term is understood to mean "repented." This is also the standard use of the term. Would it be appropriate to speak of God repenting? Rashi suggests a slightly different reading of the word in this context. God **changes intention concerning the evil** that had been announced for Nineveh, **and turns from it.**

Chapter Four

1. ***"Vayaira el Yonah, It was evil to Jonah."*** For Rashi the "evil" is Jonah's fear that the Ninevites will misunderstand the situation. Rather than recognizing that their own repentance moved God to cancel the decree of destruction they will conclude that Jonah does not in fact speak for God. Jonah **says, "Now,** that Nineveh has not been destroyed, **the idolaters, the Ninevites, will say that I am a false prophet."** Rashi resists those who would understand this verse to be an expression of Jonah's disappointment and damaged pride that God's mercy had caused the destruction described in Jonah's words not to come to pass.

2. ***"Halo zeh d'vari, Is this not my word?"*** Jonah says, **"I knew that if they returned** to You **in repentance You would not destroy** them **and I would become a liar in their eyes."**

6. ***"Vay'man, And He designated."*** This verb is the same word used at the beginning of chapter two in connection with the big fish. It should be understood as **words of invitation,** that is, God summoned the plant.

   "L'hatzil lo meira'ato, To save him from his evil." The question here is from what was Jonah saved? **From the heat of the sun.**

   "Kikayon." **A large plant with many branches** and leaves **which provides much shade, thus its name.** Perhaps his last phrase refers to Hebrew word *kanah*, used in Ezekiel 40:5 for branch or rod.

7. ***"Vatach*, Attacked."*** *Hatola'at vatach,* **The worm** *attacked,* **the plant. In place of saying this with the masculine form,** *hatola vayach,* **it uses the feminine form,** *hatola'at* **vatach.** The root Taf, Lamed, Eyin, appears in both masculine and feminine forms to mean worm.

8. ***Charishit.*** The Targum understands this word to mean, "quieting". Rashi explains, **Our sages taught that at the time when** this wind **blows it silences all other winds.** It is stronger than all other winds. In contemporary terms, it dominates the weather pattern.

   Vayitalaf "pashm'yor" **in the vernacular,** Old French.

10. ***Lo-amalta bo, You did not care for."*** The tasks included in the term *"amalta"* which Jonah did not perform: **in plowing, planting, and watering.**

   "Ben lailah, son of a night." The plant is **like the son of a** single **night for it did not grow except during one night.**

11. "*Asher lo yada, **who do not know** their right hand from their left*" refers to **children** who are too young to have yet learned this distinction. They would have been killed in the destruction of Nineveh.

*B'heimah, **Large animals**.*" This term contrasts to the previous phrase to refers to **grown adults whose thinking is like that of animals who do not know who created them.**

2 Abraham Ibn Ezra

INTRODUCTION TO THE COMMENTARY
OF ABRAHAM IBN EZRA

ABRAHAM IBN EZRA'S LIFE (c. 1092–1167) bridged the Muslim and Christian worlds. He was born in Muslim Spain and moved to Christian Italy in the middle of his life, fleeing the fundamentalist Almohades dynasty. He brought learning previously published in Arabic to the Christian world. In his commentary he draws on the Geonim and others who lived in the Arabic-speaking world.

In addition to his commentary on the books of the Hebrew Bible, Ibn Ezra wrote on Hebrew grammar, philosophy, astronomy, and poetry.

Ibn Ezra is rigorous in his analysis. He makes use of a careful reading of the grammar of individual words. He avoids fanciful midrashic interpretation. His comments are often terse. He expects much from his readers. Of all the commentators contained in this volume, he requires the most explanation.

Ibn Ezra indicates words from other places in the Tanach that will illuminate the meaning of the word in Jonah, but does not explain the connection. He leaves that to the reader. Since many of the people reading this translation will not have the background in Hebrew grammar to make the connections, I supply that explanation.

In ways Ibn Ezra seems quite modern in his theology and in his manner of reading the text. He offers support for religious pluralism in the final portion of his comment to 1:2. There he presents his understanding of the Ninevites as monotheists who previously had a proper relationship with the One God of Israel. He reads some biblical images as metaphors describing

God and God's actions in the world. He understands that one does not have to read the sequence of the verses as containing the sequence of action. We will see this in his comments to verses 1:9, 1:13 and 4:5

At times he addresses the meaning of the entire verse rather than the word at the beginning of his comment.

Abraham Ibn Ezra's Commentary to the Book of Jonah

Chapter One

1. **This is the prophet who prophesied to** the King **Jeroboam ben Yoash, as is written** about **him "that The Eternal spoke through his servant Jonah ben Amittai from Gat-Hepher"** (2 Kings 14:25). Here Ibn Ezra not only identifies our Jonah ben Ammitai with the one mentioned in 2 Kings, he also concludes that the events described there preceded the events described here.

One can wonder how there arose in the heart of a wise man, who knew God and His deeds, the thought to flee from before Him. For he, Jonah, was **in His,** God's, **hand.** Jonah was already a prophet, a servant of God. **And all** the world **is filled with His Glory.** Jonah understands that God's power and presence are not limited to the Land of Israel but rather include all creation. **And how does he prophesy** a **rebellion** against the **word of God? For it is written that he is "the prophet"** (2 Kings 14:25). Ibn Ezra states the terms of the problem. The Bible has already told us in 2 Kings that Jonah is a prophet. And here God calls Jonah to go to Nineveh and prophesy. How can it be that a prophet does not act when God calls?

One possible solution to this problem is to claim that the words in this verse do not constitute a formal call to prophecy. **And the Gaon,** Saadia, focusing on the word *k'ra,* **says, for** in the text it says "**Go to Nineveh . . . and,** *k'ra,* **proclaim over her." Does this not recall a verse like "***kir'en,* **Call to him, and he will eat bread"** (Exod 2:20). This verse is from the first encounter between Moses and his future wife, Tziporah. In this verse, Tziporah's father, there called Reuel, responds to the story of the stranger protecting his daughters at the well by telling them to invite him to come and eat with them. The word Reuel uses for invite is *kir'en.* The Gaon's point is that *k'ra* does not in fact refer to prophecy but rather to an *invitation.* Therefore, Jonah did not flee from his task as a prophet. For his instructions from God did not specifically refer to prophecy, but rather to inviting or calling the Ninevites. Here, in chapter one, God does not tell Jonah what to say to the Ninevites. The words of prophecy are not given to Jonah until chapter three.

And I say this verse, here in the book of Jonah, **is not like that** verse, there in the book of Exodus. **For there is no reason to remember if he**, Moses, **ate or did not eat,** or **if he**, Reuel, **called him or only encountered him and spoke to him.** In response to the Gaon's interpretation, Ibn Ezra points out that in the Exodus section, the word *k'ra* is incidental to what the text is telling us. And here in the book of Jonah, the use of the word *k'ra* is not peripheral to the action. Whether or not Reuel called Moses to eat with his family or just bumped into him and brought him home for dinner is a minor detail. What Jonah says to the people of Nineveh is central to the story. Therefore, we should not apply the meaning of the word *kra,* as it is used in Exodus, to our text here, in Jonah.

The Gaon's way out of the problem of how could Jonah have ignored a direct instruction to prophesy is to argue from the use of *kra* that here in verse 1 that Jonah is not told to prophesy therefore Jonah is not guilty of fleeing from the task of prophesying. Having rejected the Gaon's maneuver, Ibn Ezra now restates the question. **And still if Jonah was filled with the word of God why did he flee? And he,** Jonah, **said** *"For I hastened to flee towards Tarshish"* (4:2).

Ibn Ezra now places Jonah's flight in the context of another prophet's reluctance to follow God's instructions. **And now we saw that** even **Moses did not want to go on his mission from God to bring His** chosen **people out** of Egypt. **And here in contrast Jonah was sent to bring repentance to Nineveh** a non-Israelite city not part of "His people." Since Jonah's task is much less important than Moses's task, his greater reluctance should not be surprising.

Turning to the Midrash, Ibn Ezra offers another explanation for Jonah's flight. **And thus say our sages**, in the Mechilta to Parshat Bo, **that it is natural** to protect the **honor of the son**, Israel, over the honor of the father, God. Jonah feared that the Ninevites would heed his call and repent from their sins. This would be in stark contrast to the Israelites who regularly ignored God's prophets and continued to sin. Israel's sinfulness would be amplified by the Ninevites willingness to repent. God would as a result grow angry with the Israelites and punish them. Or one could say that the reputation of Israel among the nations would be diminished. Therefore Jonah disobeyed the father, God, to protect the son, Israel.

And now I will hint at a secret. There are those who create poetry, speak in prophesy, **in their generation without learning and there are those who require learning. And when he will receive** prophecy **in this manner,** without learning, **it is possible that he will not receive** it, meaning he will not able to comprehend it. **And it is easier for the latter ,** those with learning, **than the prior,** those without learning, to receive prophecy and prophesy. Jonah could be seen as such a prophet who receives prophecy without learning, therefore, has a difficult time receiving it and prophesying.

And in the case of **all prophets, except for Moses, after the passing of the glory of God over his face, their prophecy was** received **entirely in visions and dreams. Therefore I have said** this **about Abraham, our father, concerning prophecy from his experience with God. "And he took the knife** to kill his son" (Gen 22:10). **His ear was opened to hear quickly** God's call that he did not have to go through with the sacrifice. This was a special case in which the message did not come to Abraham in a vision or a dream because time was of the essence. The message had to be quick and clear in order to prevent Abraham from taking Isaac's life. In contrast to Moses and this one moment in Abraham's life, Jonah's communication with God was like all other prophets, in a dream or vision.

And when I searched all of Scripture I could not find the word b'richah, flee, **except connected to the word** pnay. **For example, "**_mi-panechah evrach,_ From you **I will flee"** (Ps 139:7) **or** "_vayivrach Yiftach mipnei achiv,_ **Jepthah fled from his brothers"** (Judg 11:3) **and here in the prophecy of Jonah I did not find that he fled mipnei, from God but rather** milifnei, **from before God.** The Hebrew letter Lamed is the key here. In the first two examples the Lamed is not used. Ibn Ezra will now provide other biblical examples of this usage which includes the Lamed. **As it is written, "Chai YHVH asher amaditi lifanav, As the Eternal lives, before whom I stand"** (2 Kgs 5:16). **And here** in the book of Jonah **each time he receives** prophecy he is described as _milifnei_ or _lifnei,_ with a Lamed, **the Eternal. And so it is** written **"And Cain went out Milifnei from before the Eternal"** (Gen 4:16). **Therefore, it follows from your face I will hide** (based on Gen 4:14), **for the face of the ground is** lifnei, **before the Eternal.** Cain had been speaking with God. Then he leaves God's presence and will no longer be engaged in conversation with God. **And in another Scriptural passage, "To enter the clefts of the rocks and the crevices in the cliffs mipnay, before, the terror of the Eternal"** (Isa 2:21). [The Isaiah citation in the Mikrot Gedolot version of Ibn Ezra does not follow the standard Isaiah text. The Mikrot Gedolot substitutes *beenkikay* for *visiphei* in describing the uneven nature of the cliffs.] This passage describes idolaters hiding in terror from before a vengeful God. Here the letter Lamed is not used to describe their relationship with God and there is no prophecy or other conversation between the idolaters and God. **And it is written "*To go with them toward Tarshish Milifnei, from before the Eternal*"** (1:3). Ibn Ezra concludes, based on these scriptural examples, that the use of the Lamed implies an intimate contact with God. In this type of meeting between a human and God, the call to prophecy occurs. Thus we should understand Jonah as fleeing from that type of meeting with God rather than seeking to hide from God. **And the enlightened will understand.** Those readers who understand the mystical tradition will comprehend this interpretation.

2. **"*Nineveh*" The capital of Assyria. Today it is destroyed. The sages of Israel in the land of Greece,** the Diaspora, **say that she,** Nineveh, was located at a place which today **is called Ortiyah and I didn't know** if this claim is true.

Ibn Ezra now comments on the last part of the verse *ki alta ra'atam l'fanai, their evil has arisen before me."* And **now,** here in chapter one, **He does not command him to say, "*In another forty days Nineveh* will be destroyed"** (3:3). In this verse God only says "**Their evil has arisen before me."**

And the explanation found in Pirke D'Rabbi Eliezer and other later sources, **that he was afraid that he would be called a false prophet when God repents from the evil**, the destruction of Nineveh, **is incorrect.** Ibn Ezra brings three arguments to support his rejection of this position.

(1) **For this is the reason that He did not tell him** what to say in Nineveh, **until the second time** he is called, after he is back on dry land. **For there, in** chapter three, **is written the proclamation which I give to you. And it is "*In another forty days* Nineveh will be destroyed."** Some commentators, following Jonah's own words (4:2), claim that Jonah fled because he knew that the Ninevites would repent in response to his words and that God would not destroy the city. Since Jonah's prediction of destruction would not come to pass people would call him a false prophet. Ibn Ezra rejects this line of reasoning for it is based on the false assumption that here in chapter one Jonah already knew what the message to the Ninevites would be. Ibn Ezra argues that Jonah's flight could not possibly be in response to his fear that he would be called a false prophet for he did not yet

know what God was going to instruct him to say in Nineveh. God does not tell him that until chapter three.

(2) **And how could the prophet rebel against the word of God as a result of his fear that the people of Nineveh would call him a false prophet? And why does this inflame him? For he does not live with them.** Why should Jonah care what the Ninevites say about him? He does not have ongoing contact with them.

(3) **And additionally the people of Nineveh were not foolish. Why would the Eternal send** this **prophecy upon them except to cause them to return to the Eternal? And if they would not repent, the decree,** which Jonah had proclaimed **upon them, would take effect** and they would be destroyed. **And didn't they know that this was the truth, that if they return to the Eternal then** the Eternal **would repent of the evil** that He intended to do to them. **Therefore how could they call him a false prophet?**

The correct understanding is what those who came before us, may their memory be a blessing, said. What upset him, Jonah, **was that they,** the Ninevites, **would escape at the detriment of Israel** by repenting to save themselves. Here Ibn Ezra refers to Rashi's comment on this verse and chapter ten of Pirke De Rabbi Eliezer.

Ibn Ezra now turns his attention to the second part of the verse, "*Nineveh ha'ir hagedola, Nineveh, the great city.*" **For here** in chapter three of the book of Jonah **we find the verse "It was a great city to God"** (3:3). Ibn Ezra uses this verse from chapter three to explain the verse here in chapter one. Both verses describe Nineveh as "'*ir gedola, a great city.*" The difference between the verses is that in chapter three the words "*Lailohim, to God*" are added. Ibn Ezra asks why does the text use the words "to God" to describe Nineveh. Could the text not simply described Nineveh as a "great city" without including "to God"? Ibn Ezra concludes that these words are included in the text to tell us **that they,** the Ninevites, **already feared the Eternal from before** the time of Jonah. He contends that the Ninevites were not idol worshipping polytheists but rather monotheists who worshipped the Eternal.

One might incorrectly conclude that **the** proper **explanation** of the phrase in chapter three **is that it was a big city and it is declared in the eyes of the Eternal for destruction. But this is not the way of the** Hebrew **language. For it is written, "My soul will grow up *b'einai Hashem*, in the eyes of the Eternal"** (1 Sam 26:24) **and not *Lashem*,** to the Eternal. **But here** in Jonah **it is written *Lailohim*,** to God. Ibn Ezra brings this verse from 1 Samuel to show that if the intent of the Jonah text was to say that "Nineveh was a great city <u>in the eyes of God</u>" there exists biblical language to express that idea clearly. The fact that the Jonah texts says, Lailohim and not *b'einai Elohim* demonstrates that the phrase must have a meaning other than "in the eyes of God."

Ibn Ezra continues to seek a clear understanding of this line from the third chapter. **And it is written, "All the nations are as nothing before Him,** they are counted by him as things of naught and vanity" (Isa 40:17). **And there is no concern if they were many.** This verse from Isaiah teaches that God does not care about the number of non-believers for "They are counted as things of naught and vanity." Therefore, the fact that God describes Nineveh here as a large city and in chapter 4:11—God specifically says that Nineveh is, *"a great city, in which there are more than a hundred and twenty thousand persons"*—demonstrates that the inhabitants were not in the category of "all the nations," pagans. For following the Isaiah verse, if they were pagans God would not count them. The fact that God counts them as many proves that they had a prior relationship with God.

Ibn Ezra here argues that the expression in chapter three of Jonah, "a great city to God," does not describe the size of Nineveh but rather its importance to God. **And the explanation** of the word *Lailohim* **is that they had been fearers of the Eternal in earlier days. Only now, in the days of Jonah did they begin to do evil. If they had not originally been people of the Eternal, a prophet would not have been sent to them. And here we saw a complete repentance with nothing like it.**

And we do not find it written that they broke the altars of Baal or cut down idols. If they had been idol worshippers turning now for the first time to the worship of the One God, their complete repentance would have included the destruction of the places of idol worship. Chapter three includes a detailed description of the steps the people of Nineveh took to repent from their evil. There is no mention of destroying altars to idols. **From this we can learn that they were not idol worshipers.** This why they merit God's attention and a visit from God's prophet.

3. **"Vayeired Yafo,** *And Jonah arose to flee to Tarshish from before The Eternal and* **he went down to Jaffa."** The Gaon, Saadia, **says that** *Tarshish* **is Tarsus but Rabbi Mvaseir,** another Gaon, **says it is Tunis in Africa.**

"Vayitein s'charah, *And he paid it's fare."* **Not all of the cost** for the entire ship, **but rather just what he was required to pay for his portion,** for the cost of one person to travel from Jaffa to Tarshish. Here Ibn Ezra responds to Rashi who argues that Jonah paid the price for the entire ship. Rashi's comment seems to be based on the image that the ship's captain waited in port until he sold all the passenger spots on his ship and only then departed. Jonah, in order to arrange for the immediate departure of the ship, bought all the seats. The word, *scharah,* has a feminine possessive suffix. Rashi understands it to refer to the ship. Ibn Ezra understands it to refer to Jonah's place on the ship.

4. **"YHVH haytil, And The Eternal cast."** Ibn Ezra explains that we should not understand this to mean that God had a container of winds from which he cast this wind. Rather we should understand the phrase to mean that "**He sent** the storm." The verb *Haytil* is used **in the manner of a metaphor. And the reason that he sent it from the land** toward the sea **is so that they would not be able to return to the land.** Ibn Ezra suggests that the word *haytil* tells us that the God sent the storm to blow in a specific direction. Because we know that the sailors were unable to bring the ship closer to the shore we can conclude that the winds and currents formed by the storm came from the direction of the land toward the open sea. **For it is not only the place where the sea joins with the river,** presumably the Yarkon, **it is close to the shore, a place that is always difficult for ships.** The area close to shore presents many problems for safe navigation including varying depths of the sea, changing tides, varying currents and the rocks of the coast. **And the evidence for this** understanding of the text **is** in chapter 2:4 **as it says, "You cast me into the depth, the heart of the sea and the river whirled around me."** Therefore, this must have been a part of the sea close enough to the mouth of a river for there still to be a river current to "whirl around" Jonah.

"**V'ha'oniya hashva, The ship thought."** We know that a ship cannot think. Ibn Ezra demonstrates that the Bible sometimes poetically describes inanimate objects as acting in a human manner. **This is similar to** the verse **"When a land sins against me"** (Ezek 14:13). Just as a land cannot actually sin so a ship cannot actually think. Both verses must be understood as presenting poetic images.

5. **"Vayir'u hamelachim, And the sailors feared."** The problem here is the use of the word *melachim.* From the context of the sentence it clearly refers to the sailors but its derivation is unclear. So Ibn Ezra tells us that it is **those who guide the ship.** He then provides a biblical verse with a similar use of the same word in a slightly different form: **"*malachayich,* your sailors and**

your pilots . . ." (Ezek 27:27). This verse from Ezekiel is describing ships from Tarshish.

And Yafet ben Ali **said, the sailor, *malach*, was causing them to move, *molichim*.** He draws a connection between our word *melachim* (with a root of Mem, Lamed, Chet) and *Molichim* (with a root of Mem, Lamed, Chaf).

"El yirkatei has'phina, To the holds of the ship." The word *yirkatei* is in a plural form. Jonah cannot be in more than one of the holds. **To one of the ship's holds.** This usage is similar another biblical verse. "**And he,** Jepthah, **was buried in the cities of Giliad**" (Judg 12:7). Clearly Jepthah was not buried in more than one place. Just as Jepthah was buried in one of the cities of Giliad, so Jonah was in one of the holds of the ship.

"Vayishkav vayirdam, "He lay down and fell asleep." **From the danger of the sea and His anger. Perhaps he did not enter the ship before this** storm began. This verse is often read to mean that Jonah was already on board and already sleeping in the hold when the storm began. Ibn Ezra suggests a different sequence of events. He says perhaps the storm was already raging and that Jonah sought to escape the fury of the storm and God's anger by going to sleep in the hold. This reading shifts Jonah from being oblivious to the severe storm to consciously hiding from it.

6. *"Vayikrav rav hachoveil, And the captain drew close."* Ibn Ezra here solves two problems, the meaning of the word *rav* and the meaning of the word *choveil*. He first explains that *rav* is the captain and then explains that *choveil* refers to the sailors. **The most prominent among the *chovlim*. He was the highest of the *chovlim*,** literally "seizers," understood here as **those who seize the mast. And Rabbi Moses** ibn Gikatilla **says, it is** derived **from the word *tachbulot*, cunning.** Both words have the same three letter root, Chet, Bet, Lamed.

"Yitashait." This Hitpa'ail verb occurs only this one time in the entire Bible. To understand it Ibn Ezra turns to related nouns which share the same three letter root (Eiyin, Shin, and Tav) found in other biblical verses. **It is like *"ivdu eshtonotav*, His thoughts perish"** (Ps 146:4). Based on this Psalms verse, our verse could then mean, "God will think" or "God will consider." Ibn Ezra now presents another related word. **And similarly** *"eshtei asar*, eleven"** (Num 7:72). The Hebrew Bible only uses *eshtei* in conjunction with *asar* to mean eleven. Since *asar*, is the very common word for "ten," then *eshtei* must mean "one." **Because this is the number it is like two accountings, general and specific.** The captain would like Jonah to

pray so that perhaps God will take account of Jonah's individual prayer and save all the sailors. **And like this** we can understand our word to mean **God takes account of me.**

7. **"*Vayomru, And they said.*"** There are those, (e.g., Rashi, following Pirke D'Rabbi Eliezer) **who say that there were other ships in the area which were able to escape** from the storm; **only this one** ship **was in trouble therefore they said "*Come let us cast lots.*"** The sailors saw that this was no ordinary storm. They understood that there must be a special supernatural reason why the storm trapped only their ship.

　"*B'shelmi, On account of whom.*" And this is similar to "*al hashel.*" (2 Sam 6:7). Both verses contain the common Hebrew word *shel* in an unusual form. In the verse in 2 Samuel, God punishes Uzzah for touching the Ark of the Covenant during its transportation to Jerusalem. The entire verse reads, "And The Eternal was angry with Uzzah, and God struck him there, *al hashel*, and he died there next to the Ark of God." The *al* means "on" or "for." From context we can conclude that *hashel* refers to Uzzah's act of touching the ark. Biblical translators render it "for his error" or "for his indiscretion" or "for his crime." Ibn Ezra understands it to mean "on account of what he did." This helps Ibn Ezra with our verse. In the word *b'shelmi* the *mi* means "whom." Drawing upon this 2 Samuel verse Ibn Ezra concludes that *b'shelmi* means "on account of whom."

8. **"*Vayomru, And they spoke.*" The commentator,** Rashi, **who explains that they,** the sailors, **want to know from what people he is, and from what land** he came **because perhaps a decree of death from heaven was issued upon them,** all the people of that land, **is not correct. For if the Eternal had decreed** death **upon that people** and if he, Jonah, **was not** currently **in one of the cities upon which the decree** was pronounced **but rather in another place with other people, why should the other** people **be frightened? As if they had included themselves in the decree pronounced on him alone to die?** Surely God could separate out the single intended target of punishment from the innocent bystanders, the sailors.

　Ibn Ezra explains that it is natural that the sailors asked Jonah about his occupation. **It is the custom of most people to have a trade. The trade of the person teaches** us **about his situation and why he enters a certain place.** Also it is natural for the sailors to have asked Jonah where is he from for **there are certain places where most of the people are good. And this is well known today.**

9. **"*Vayomer, And he said.*"** In verse eight the sailors ask Jonah many questions. He does not answer them in the order in which they were asked. **He responds to them concerning the last** question. He tells them he is an *"Evri."* Ibn Ezra explains the source of the use of the term *Evri* to describe the Israelites. **He is from the sons of Eber who are called** *Evri.* **For they follow the faith of the original Eber,** monotheism. **"For he is the father of all the children of Eber"** (Gen 10:21). Genesis 11:16–26 lists the generations from Eber to Abraham, showing that Abraham, and hence all Israelites, are descendants of Eber, biologically and spiritually.

He was in awe only of the Eternal from before whom he fled. Jonah's flight should not be seen as a rejection of God's power. Nor did Jonah believe that God's power was limited to the Land of Israel. **And he,** Jonah, in the second half of this verse, **proclaimed** that God formed **the heavens, the earth and the sea and he reasons, "For I know that He acts and will rule over it all."**

10. **"*Vayiru, And they feared.*"** Ibn Ezra explains why the sailors were filled with fear of the Eternal. **In response to his,** Jonah's, **statement,** in the previous verse, *"The Eternal, the God of heaven* **I fear."** **And they said to him, "What is this?** What is your **reason** to fear? **How could you flee from before the Eternal?"** The sailors challenge Jonah. You yourself proclaim the Eternal's power, how could you flee?

Ibn Ezra now responds to the problem of the sequence of the verse. At the beginning of the verse the sailors express their fear. But their fear does not make sense unless they know the story of Jonah's flight. In this verse, first we read of their fear and then we read that Jonah told them his story. **For he had revealed his secret to them.** Ibn Ezra explains that we should understand the verb "*higid, told*" as meaning "he <u>had</u> told." That is, Jonah had already told the sailors of his story, therefore they were afraid.

11. **"*Mah na'aseh, What should we do?*"** **And the reason** that the sailors ask Jonah, "What should we do to you?" is because they want direction from the person who understands the ways of the Eternal. They say, **"Give us advice as to what to do."**

"*Vayishtok hayam, And the sea was quiet.*" This is similar to *vayismchu vayishtiku,* **They were glad when they were quiet"** (Ps 107:30). In the Psalms verse we have the same word as in the Jonah verse used to describe a quieting sea after a big storm. In the Psalms verse, God has brought a big storm, the people have cried out to God and God has saved them by quieting the storm. This is what the sailors want to see happen to them. They are seeking Jonah's advice as how to cry out to God.

12. **"Vayomeir, And he said." He desired and requested to die.** Jonah does speak of repenting of his sin and seeking to resume his life as a prophet. Rather he prefers death so that he would **not** be required to **draw the Ninevites back to the Eternal.** As Ibn Ezra explained in comment to verse one, Jonah wanted to protect the honor of Israel. He feared that if he would prophesy to the Ninevites, they would repent of their sins. Thereby bringing shame upon the Israelites who never repent of their sins in response to the call of the prophets. Jonah would rather give up his own life then bring shame upon Israel. **And he did not say this to them,** the sailors, **so that he would not hear from their mouths that they would send him** to Nineveh. He was concerned that if he explained to the sailors the entire situation they would not seek to quiet the sea by killing Jonah but rather by sending him on his mission to Nineveh.

13. **"Vayacht'ru, And they dug."** Ibn Ezra first explains that this verb refers to completed action. The sailors had already completed the futile attempt to return to shore. **Its meaning is that they had already "rowed."** The point is that the attempt to row to shore described in verse 13 did not take place after the conversation contained in verses 11 and 12 but rather took place before the events described in verse 11 and 12. The sailors first response to the crisis would have been to try to row back to shore. When that failed they turned to extraordinary measures.

Ibn Ezra now turns to the use of this word particular to describe rowing. While other Hebrew words could have been used. *Vayacht'ru* is a more poetic way of expressing the idea. **And the word "Vayacht'ru,"** which generally means digging, **is used because the rowers are similar to diggers.** As diggers place their shovels in the soil and pull so oarsmen place their oars in the water and pull.

14. **"Vayikr'u, And they called."** Why did these non-Israelite sailors call out to the Eternal, the God of Israel? **They all believed in the Eternal One of Glory.** Because of their experience with Jonah and the storm, they have become believers in "the Eternal One of Glory." **And they turned** to Him **to call upon Him** in prayer.

"B'nefesh, In the life of this man." **On account** of. This unusual usage of the preposition Bet **is similar to "And Jacob served on account of**

Rachel, *b'rachel,* seven years" (Gen 29:20). In both cases the preposition Bet is understood not as meaning "in" but rather "on account of."

"Ka'asher chafatzta, As You wished." This is an expression **that it was clear to them,** the sailors, **that on his,** Jonah's, **account the sea was storming.** They recognize that the storm was not a normal natural occurrence but rather an act of God in response to Jonah's flight. Before they throw Jonah into the sea they proclaim out loud that they do this only in response to God's will. They believe that Jonah will die as a result of their action. They do not want to be seen as murders but rather as people obeying God's will.

15. *"Mizapo, From its raging."* It is **in the manner of a metaphor.** Describing a sea as raging is such common English usage we might not even consider it a metaphor. The word occurs in the Bible thirteen times. This is the only place that is used to describe the sea. Everywhere else it is used to describe a person or God. Ibn Ezra provides one example. **And it,** this word, **is similar** in meaning **to *"zoaphim,* Raging"** (Gen 40:6). There it is used to describe the troubled state of Pharaoh's butler and baker the morning after their dreams.

16. *"Vayizb'chu, And they offered* an *offering."* The text tells us that the sailors offered sacrifices to the Eternal, but it does not tell us when or how. The reader might conclude that they offered the sacrifices immediately after the storm stopped. This image raises many problems, including what did they have on board to sacrifice? Ibn Ezra explains that they offered a sacrifice **after they left the ship.**

Chapter Two

1. *"Vay'man, And He designated."* **This is similar to** *zimun,* **summon.** *"Va'yahi Yonah, And Jonah was* in the belly of the fish." **A person does not have the strength to live in the belly of a fish for even an hour and for this number** of days it is **only possible by the means of a miracle.** Ibn Ezra rejects the approach of those who try to join together natural events and the story of Jonah. He says that those who want to discuss which species of fish are large enough to accommodate a person for three days are not only incorrect, they also miss the point of this story.

2. *"Vayitpalail, And he prayed."* The central section of chapter 2:3–10, contains Jonah's prayer. At the end of the chapter, in verse 11, God commands

the fish to return Jonah to dry land. Ibn Ezra reports a dispute among biblical commentators concerning the timing of this prayer. Ibn Ezra believes that the sequence of the chapter reflects the sequence of events. Other commentators argue that Jonah did not recite the prayer until he was already back on dry land. **The commentators wish to explain** the text by means of a **new idea and remove the text from its plain meaning by saying that Jonah did not pray until after he had gone out** of the fish and **onto dry land.** They base this interpretation on the preposition, *mem,* which **they found** preceding the word for "belly." Since the text reads *"mim'ei, from the belly"* not *"b'ma'ei, in the belly."* They argue that Jonah must have already been saved "from the belly" when he prayed. **Did they not see that there in the text,** in verse three, it is written, '*Mibetten . . . shivati,* From the belly . . . I cried out." This is similar to "From the depths I cried out to God" (Ps 110:1). **Additionally the word** *"shivati,* I cried out" is a sign that he prayed and cried out before the fish vomited him. And similarly** in verse 8 of this chapter Jonah uses the future tense to describe his prayer reaching God "**My prayer will come before you.**" **And** if these commentators are correct **why is it not written here** in verse 2, **"And Jonah prayed after he went out of the belly of the fish?" In addition after his prayer it is written "And the Eternal spoke to the fish** and it spit Jonah out on to dry land" (2:11). Ibn Ezra argues that the text clearly places these two events, the prayer and the return to land, in proper sequence. **For** God **brought him into this difficult** situation **in order to save** him **from sin.** God provides Jonah with the opportunity to repent and seek forgiveness. And in response to his situation Jonah declares **"My prayer <u>will</u> come before you"** (2:8).

Another basis for arguing that Jonah recited the prayer after his deliverance is that the verbs in the prayer are in the past tense. For example, in verse 3 Jonah says, "*karati,* I called." Ibn Ezra responds, **and now pay attention and see that all the prayers of a prophet and his blessings were in the spirit of prophecy.** Ibn Ezra now provides a number of examples in which the Bible uses past tense verbs to describe events that have not yet taken place. He argues that these words are said in "the spirit of prophecy." So these events are understood as events which without a doubt will take place, therefore they are spoken of in the past tense as if they had already occurred. **"And Jacob said,' I <u>took</u> from the hand of the Amorites** with my sword and my bow" (Gen 48:22). In the blessing of Joseph's sons, Jacob speaks of what their descendants will one day inherit. This "taking of the land of the Amorites" does not occur until the time of Joshua, nevertheless

Jacob uses the past tense to describe it. **For an event which has been decreed** by God **to happen, can be spoken of in the past tense. In a similar manner, "and he bow<u>ed</u> his shoulder to bear** and become a slave in forced labor" (Gen 49:15). This is Jacob's blessing of Issachar, again describing in the past tense events that will not occur until after the conquest of the land. Another example, **"A star <u>came</u> forth out of Jacob** and a scepter arose out of Israel" (Num 24:17). This is from Baalam's words concerning the Israelites. He is describing the future, probably the reign of King David, using past tense verbs.

"But Jeshurun wax<u>ed</u> fat and kick<u>ed</u>" (Deut 32:15) and **"And God saw it and spurn<u>ed</u> them"** (Deut 32: 19). These are words from the Song of Moses, through which Moses tells the story of the people of Israel including the future events which will befall the people of Israel. Again in both verses we see past tense verbs. **"So Israel <u>dwelt</u> in safety"** (Deut 33:28). This verse is from the final blessing which Moses recites just before his death. He is describing the future of the people, when they will turn away from sin, using past tense verbs. **And in the prayer of David "in his flight"** (Ps 3:1). from Absalom his son. **"And He answer<u>ed</u> me from His holy mountain"** (Ps 3:5). **For the text says "<u>in</u> his flight."** While David was still fleeing from Absalom he speaks in the past tense of his salvation, that is to come. The text, **does not say, "he fled** from Absalom **and in his prayer** he said . . . ," for that wording would leave open the possibility that this entire section was composed after the David had been saved from Absalom. The Psalms line as we have it provides a final example of a future event described with a past tense verb.

To conclude his case for understanding the prayer to have been recited in the belly of the fish, Ibn Ezra draws upon two excerpts from the prayer itself. *"Ach osif l'habit el haichal kodshecha, But I will look again at your holy palace"* (2:5). **This is the sky.** Rashi says that the words "holy palace" refer to the Temple in Jerusalem. And that Jonah is speaking of again being able to see the Temple in Jerusalem. "I see now that you have kept me alive all these days therefore I know that I will again gaze at your Holy Temple." Ibn Ezra explains that Jonah in the belly of the fish is not thinking about seeing the Temple in Jerusalem but rather surviving his ordeal and again seeing the sky. Ibn Ezra draws upon a verse from Psalms to show that in the Bible, God's "holy palace" is understood to be in the heavens. **"For the Eternal is in His holy palace,** His throne is in the heavens" (Ps 11:4). The second half of the verse locates God's throne in the heavens, if we assume that the throne is in the palace, we can conclude that God's palace is in the heavens. **And Rabbi** Yehudah Halevi explains it **in this manner.** If "Holy palace" refers to the Temple in Jerusalem then these words could have been spoken by Jonah after his return to dry land. If the phrase refers to the sky, it could only have been said from the belly of the fish.

And there, in verse 10, **it is written, "Salvation from the Eternal."** In this concluding phrase of Jonah's prayer, he speaks of offering sacrifices in fulfillment of his vows and in response to God's act of salvation. The problem, which Ibn Ezra addresses, is that if the prayer was recited while Jonah was still in the fish's belly the salvation had not yet taken place when Jonah spoke. According to Ibn Ezra's understanding "salvation from the Eternal" is not what has already taken place. But rather **this was his hope. "Salvation from the Eternal" is what he was seeking.**

Ibn Ezra now turns to the problem of the gender of the fish. In verse 1 the fish is called *dag,* which is the masculine form. In verse 2 the fish is called *daga,* which is the feminine form. Rashi solves this problem by explaining that the story involves two fish—a *dag,* a masculine fish, and a *daga,* a feminine fish. "It was a male fish and he could stand in an open space and so he was not moved to pray. The Holy Blessed One intimated to the male fish and it spit him into the mouth of a female fish which was full of embryos. There he was stressed and he prayed there, as it says *mimayei hadaga,* from the belly of the female fish." Ibn Ezra responds, **There is a person who says that the feminine fish swallowed** him from the mouth of **the masculine fish. There is no need for this** complex explanation. **For Dag and Daga are nouns** without distinction as to **gender, like *tzedek* and** *tzedakah* (righteousness/justice)**.** They can be used interchangeably.

3. *Sheol* **a deep dark place which is the opposite of the heavens which are on high.** Jonah is as distant from God as a person can be.

4. *"Yamim, Seas."* Ibn Ezra explains why the text uses the plural form of the word even though it is clear that Jonah is only in one sea. **It is like "*al yoraihem, on your Niles"* (Exod 7:19). As there is only one Nile, there in the book of Exodus, so there is only one sea here, in the book of Jonah.

And Yafet ben Ali **says that the Sea of Reeds mixes with the Sea of Yaffo.** Yafet ben Ali proposes a different understanding of the phrase. He suggests that the plural form, *"yamim, seas,"* is used because the spot at which Jonah was thrown into the water was the convergence of two seas, the Sea of Reeds and the Sea of Yaffo. **And the** word **reeds is similar to "She**

placed him in the reeds" (Exod 2:3) **so that he,** Moses, **would be close** to the shore.

5. *"Nigrashti mineged einecha, I was driven from before your eyes";* **that being the heavens.** Jonah is under water in the belly of the fish and cannot see the heavens. The problem here is that one might think that this word, *nigrashti,* refers to Jonah's flight from before God's presence. The word however is in a passive form so that in cannot refer to an action of Jonah, but rather something that happened to him, i.e., being thrown into the sea. So he can describe himself as driven under water away from God's eyes.

6. *"Ad nefesh, Until my soul."* **Until my soul was about to die.**

7. *"L'kitzvai, Cutoff."* The text uses an unusual word to describe the base of the mountains, **to the place where the mountains are** <u>cutoff.</u> This is **from the category** of phrases such as, **and he** <u>cut a tree</u> at its base.

    "V'haaretz, The Land." The text says, *"The land, its bars against me forever."* Ibn Ezra explains that the text must be read with the words "are closed," which come from the context of the sentence. Jonah thought, the land, **its bars** <u>are closed</u> **against me, I will not be able to get out** and again **be on dry land.**

8. *B'hit'ateif, In wrapping."* Ibn Ezra points out a biblical use of another form of the same root (Eiyen, Tet , Fay) to refer to fainting. **This is similar to "***Ya'atof,* **as he was faint"** (Ps 102:1).

    "V'ta'al mishachat chayai, You lifted my life from the pit." This phrase is from the end of verse 7. Ibn Ezra uses it to explain the word *nafshi, my soul,* in verse 8. **This is in the manner of metaphor concerning** <u>his soul</u> **that in truth is** <u>his life.</u> Ibn Ezra's task is to explain what "soul" in verse eight refers to when it says, *"my soul was faint within me."* Ibn Ezra connects *chayai, my life,* from verse 7, with *nafshi, my soul,* from verse 8. And concludes that Jonah felt himself to be close to death.

9. *"M'shamrim, They guarded."* The question here concerns the form of the verb. The text could have used the more common form of this root *shomrim* in the *Kal* conjugation but rather uses *m'shamrim* in the *Pi'ail* conjugation. Ibn Ezra explains this is an **intense verb which stresses that the men of the ship were calling out and encouraging one another** in their acts of idolatry. The sailors did not simply maintain their idolatrous worship they "zealously guarded" it.

Now the word "*Chasdam, Their kindness.*" Ibn Ezra explains why the word has the possessive suffix *am*, their, rather than appearing in the text as *chesed*. **They had thought that they had done an act of** *chesed*, **kindness,** when they threw Jonah into the sea. Therefore the word used is "*chasdam*, their kindness." **Or the explanation could be that** rather than referring to "their kindness" it means "this kindness" **this is similar to "*chesed hu*, this kindness"** (Mic 7:18).

10. "*Asher nidarti, that I swore.*" The text does not explicitly mention Jonah uttering a formal vow which he is now declaring he will fulfill. Ibn Ezra explains that Jonah is referring to all **that I swore in the belly of the fish,** all the promises of devotion to God that Jonah expresses in his prayer.

11. "*Vayomeir, And He said.*" The text says that "God spoke." Are we to understand that God spoke words which the fish heard? No. **In the manner of a metaphor** "He spoke" means that **He compelled him,** the fish, **to fulfill the Divine wishes.**

Chapter Three

1. "*Vayahi, And* the word of *The Eternal was.*" God speaks to Jonah **a second time.**

2. "*Kum, Arise.*" **It teaches that he,** Jonah after the fish spit him onto dry land, **did not travel on a path that took him far from Nineveh.** So that **if** God **would send him a second time he would** be able to **go** quickly. After his experiences at sea and in the fish, Jonah was fully prepared to respond to God's call to deliver prophecy to Nineveh.

3. "*Vayakom, Jonah arose.*" **Rabbi Joshua said that the men of the ship went to Nineveh and told them the story of Jonah and therefore they had faith** in the Eternal. Ibn Ezra explains why Jonah reacts positively to this second call from God. When he arrives in Nineveh, he knows he will not seen as a strange unknown Israelite. Rather he will be a person whose reputation precedes him. He can expect that the people of Nineveh will respond to his words having already heard the testimony of the sailors.

And the word "*Leilohim, To God.*" **I have already explained,** in the comment to 1:2.

"Mahalach shloshet yamim, A **walk of three days."** Some people understand verses 3 and 4 to mean that the city of Nineveh was a three days walk across and that Jonah walked for one day straight into the city before he spoke. A city that was so large that it would take three days to walk across would be unbelievably large even by modern standards. Ibn Ezra explains that this description is not of the diameter of the city but rather the circumference of the entire district. It would take three days to walk **around the district**. The one day's walk in verse 4 should not be understood as walking straight into the city, for he would emerge from the other side before the day was done. Rather it could mean **that he walked one day from one side to the other** speaking as he went to the Ninevites he encountered **or** it could mean **that when he walked** to Nineveh **to give his proclamation** from where God spoke to him **it was a one day walk to get there.**

4. *"Vayachel, And Jonah* **started."** **There are those who say it means reversed, that is it,** the city of Nineveh, **had reversed,** turned away from, **its evil deeds** before Jonah spoke. **But this explanation is not correct.** Ibn Ezra points to a section from the book of Jeremiah where that prophet faces a similar situation to the one Jonah faces here. **Rather this word is similar to the expression "In a moment I will speak** concerning a nation and concerning a kingdom, to pluck up and break down and to destroy it. But if that nation turns from their evil, because of which I have spoken against it, I repent of the evil that I thought to do unto it" (Jer 18:7–8). *"Vayachel"* at the beginning of the Jonah verse is similar to the words, *"rega adabair,* In a moment I will speak," at the beginning of the Jeremiah passage, meaning that Jonah is preparing to speak to the people of Nineveh.

5. *"Vaya'aminu, And* the people of Nineveh **believed."** This is similar to **"And the nation believed" (Exod** 4:31**).** There, in the book of Exodus, the people of Israel respond to Moses and believed. Here the people of Nineveh respond to Jonah and believe *"Beilohim, In God."* **In the word of God.** Ibn Ezra explains that what is reported here is not an abstract theological statement that the Ninevites believed in the existence of the God of Israel. But rather that they believed the words of the God of Israel as spoken by Jonah were true and that Nineveh was about to be destroyed.

6. *"Vayiga, And the word* **reached."** **This is before the people put on sack cloth.** Ibn Ezra explains that the sequence of the verses in this section does not match the sequence of events as they actually took place. The acts of repentance described in the second half of verse 5 did not take place until

after the king's response described in verses 6 through 9. In Ibn Ezra's approach to the text the people put on sack cloth and fast in response to the king's decree.

"*Vaya'aveir. And he passed.*" The king **removed** his royal garments.

"*Vayachas, And he covered.*" The text does not provide an object for the verb. Ibn Ezra points out that the object of the verb can be understood from context of the sentence. He covered **his flesh with the sackcloth.** Ibn Ezra explains that an object is necessary **for this is a Yotzei**, an active, as opposed to a stative, **verb** which requires the preposition *et* and an object.

7. "*Mita'am, From the reasoning.*" **From his advice, his knowledge and his wisdom. And this is similar to "in changing his discernment"** (Ps 34:1). This Psalms verse refers to an incident in 1 Samuel 21:14f in which David "feigns madness" during his flight from Saul. David changes his discernment, or judgment, to appear to be crazy. It is this sense of *ta'am* as judgment that Ibn Ezra applies to our verse.

8. "*Vayik'r'u, And he called.*" The question here is who is the subject of this verb, who "called" out to God? At the beginning of the sentence we read of people and animals. From the structure of the sentence one might conclude that people and animals called out to God. Ibn Ezra makes it clear that this second clause refers to a **person. Whether he is the son of knowledge**, rational **or he is one who knows he did wrong,** has moral judgment.

(There is a problem here with the printed text of Ibn Ezra's commentary. What appears here following comment on verse 8, is a fragment of a comment on verse 9. We would expect to find the Hebrew letter Tet, 9, indicating a new verse and then the word or phrase Ibn Ezra wishes to explain. Since he comments on every verse we cannot conclude that he simply skips verse 9. In the printed edition the problem occurs between where the commentary stops on one page and is resumed on the next page. We can conclude that the beginning of the comment to verse 9 and perhaps the end of the comment were left out of the printed edition. This gap also exists in the Vatican manuscript version of Ibn Ezra.)

Or this is similar to and perhaps (This fragment could be part of the end of the comment on verse 8 or the beginning of the comment on verse 9 or it could be divided between the two verses. "Or this is similar to" could be an introduction to a proof text which is missing from the printed edition.)

The word "*Vashav,* turned", refers to The glorious Eternal who turned away from his anger and did not destroy Nineveh.

10. "*Vayar Haelohim, God saw* their deeds, that they repented." The question Ibn Ezra answers is what specifically did God see? For one can not see repentance. God saw **that they believed in him. And so it is in** the weekly Torah portion **Yitro,** where the text says *"Lifnei Haelohim,* **before God"** (Exod 18:12). In this section of the book of Exodus, Jethro the father in law of Moses, a non-Israelite comes to meet Moses in the wilderness after the exodus. He hears from Moses of God's acts of redemption. Jethro praises God's redemptive power and offers a sacrifice to the God. Ibn Ezra argues that the devotion of the Ninevites here is similar to the devotion of Jethro there. What did God see? The Ninevites offering sacrifices to the One God as Jethro had done.

"*Vayinachem, And He repented.*" The text describes God as "repenting." Repenting is a important and necessary human activity. One we would not associate with God. Ibn Ezra explains that this the text uses this image because **the Torah speaks in the language of people.** So that people will be able to understand it.

Chapter Four

1. "*Vayayra, It was evil.*" Jonah was displeased **because God repented.**

2. "*Vatitpalail, And he prayed.*" **His,** Jonah's, **explanation** for his anger is explained in this prayer.

"*V'nicham, Relented.*" To understand this phrase one must first establish how to view this word grammatically. Is it a past tense verb referring to God's action in having relented from the destruction of Nineveh. Or is it a participle acting as an adjective referring to God as relenting of evil, completing the list of adjectives describing God's nature. **It is an adjective, this is why it has a Kamatz** under the Chet, **following the rules for the Nifal conjugation.** In the Nifal we find a Kamatz under the second letter of the root in the participle of the masculine singular form. In the past tense masculine singular form, the word would also Nicham but it would have a Patach under the Chet instead of the Kamatz found here in our text.

3. *"V'ata, And now."* **Since he sees that Israel will not repent, he fears that evil will befall them. Therefore he prays, *"Take my soul"* in the manner of be kind to me. This is similar to what Elisha did in his anointing of Chaza'ail.** Chaza'ail was a King of Aram who God sent to attack the Israelites as a punishment for misdeeds. Earlier God instructs Elijah to anoint Chaza'ail as king (1 Kgs 19:15). Elijah does not complete this task during his remaining days on earth. Elisha carries on for him. When Elisha comes to anoint Chaza'ail as king he cries for he understands that this person will be God's agent to bring suffering on the Israelites (2 Kgs 8:7f.). So here in our text Jonah is upset because he realizes that God will now use the Ninevites to destroy the Northern Kingdom.

4. *"Haheiteiv"* **This is similar to "I . . . crushed it, *heitaiv*, grinding it finely"** (Deut 9:21). **This grinding is full and complete.** This verse from Deuteronomy describes the destruction of the Golden Calf. Ibn Ezra points out that in the Deuteronomy verse the word *heiteiv* is used to explain the full extent of the grinding process. Therefore, we can see that here in our verse it is used to explain the full depth of Jonah's despair.

And what is **the reason** God asks **why are you upset about this? Yafet ben Ali says** that God's question should be understood as meaning, **it angers you that I am good to those to whom I want** to be good? **This is vanity!** God's question in this verse is not an inquiry by which God seeks information concerning Jonah's emotional state. But rather it is an expression of God's amazement at Jonah's self-centered attitude.

5. *"Vayeitzei, And he went out."* Why does this verse begin with the word "Vayeitzei, he went out?" Surely Jonah left Nineveh immediately after issuing his proclamation contained in verse 4 of chapter three. The text **returns to the earlier moment in the story to recall the words of Jonah which he proclaimed before the completion of the forty days.** The sequence of the verses in this chapter does not follow the sequence of events as they unfolded. The conversation between God and Jonah described in verses 1–4 took place after Jonah's departure from Nineveh described here in verse 5.

Ibn Ezra now supplies examples of similar usages of this construction from other parts of the Bible. **In the manner of "And he came to the place"** (Gen 28:11). This verse describes the arrival of Jacob at Bethel, the site of his famous dream, during his journey from Canaan to Paddan-aram. The problem is that earlier in the chapter, in verse five, the text reads, "he went to Paddan-aram." This suggests he left Canaan and arrived in Paddan-aram.

Then in verse 11 Jacob is not in Paddan-aram but rather back in middle of his journey. **Also "Joseph took the two of them"** (Gen 48:13). This verse is from the story of Jacob blessing Joseph's two sons, Menasseh and Ephraim. This verse says "Joseph <u>took</u>" even though in verse one of the same chapter the text already says that Joseph "<u>took</u> his two sons." In these two Genesis verses we have verbs recalling events which had already taken place. In a similar manner Vayaytzei in our verse recalls Jonah's departure from Nineveh which also had already taken place. Ibn Ezra understands that the events described in 4:1–4 took place after Jonah's departure from Nineveh described in verse 5.

6. **"*Kikayon.*" The sages of Spain say that it is a *dala'at,* a gourd, or a *kara.*** It is unknown to which type of plant this word refers. **And there is no need to know what it is.** Knowing the precise type of plant would not add to our understanding of the events of the story.

"*L'hatzil lo meira'ato, to save him from his suffering.*" **From most of the heat of the sun. There are those who say that because he stood in the belly of the fish for a long time the skin of his flesh was tender and could not with stand the heat.** This approach explains why Jonah required more protection from the sun than would most other people.

7. **"*L'macharat,* the next day."** Meaning the day after **the day of his joy in the *kikayon* plant.** Ibn Ezra explains that only one day passed from the appearance of the plant described in verse six and its destruction described in verse seven.

8. **"*Ruach Kadim.*" A wind from the east.**

"*Charishit, Deafening.*" **Rabbi Merinos,** Rabbi Yonah ibn Janach, **said that is was so strong that hearing its roar deafened the ears.** The root of this word is Chet, Raish, Shin, which can mean silent or deaf. We should not mistakenly conclude that the wind was silent. Quite the opposite, it was so strong it was deafening.

"*Vayitalaf.*" This word can be understood in two ways. Ibn Ezra first points out a biblical example of its use to mean "faint". **This is similar to "*titalafna,* they shall faint"** (Amos 8:13). Then he provides a biblical example of its use meaning "wrapped." **"And she put on a veil *vatitalaf,* <u>wrapping</u> herself up"** (Gen 38:14). He now explains the connection between the two meanings of the word as used in our verse. **He,** Jonah, **grew faint wrapped in his clothes.**

9. **"*Vayomeir, And He said.*"** Why does God continue to speak with Jonah who is so disappointing a prophet? **The Eternal continues to teach his prophet even though he angers Him because the Eternal is gracious.**

10. **"*Vayomeir, And He said.*"** Ibn Ezra explains why God uses the plant and the worm to make this point to Jonah. **The text speaks in this manner so that all who hear it** will know **that, does not the Eternal labor on behalf of all his creations?** Speaking to Jonah, God asks, **And this is the reason you took pity on this thing for which you did nothing?** If you feel pity for this plant, **how can I not take pity on all** the results **of my acts,** all of my creatures?

And the word *bin* with a Chirik, instead of its more common vowel, a Segol, **is similar to "*bin*, the son of Nun"** (Num 13:8). **"And if the wicked man, *bin hakot,* deserves lashes"** (Deut 25:2). In all three cases one would expect to find a Segol, under the Bet, but the text uses a Chirik without affecting the meaning of the word.

Did he not rejoice in the plant for only one day from the morning until the evening? And understand that it grew up from the beginning of the night until the morning. It lived for the day light hours of that one day **until the evening when it fell and dried up completely before the dawn. This** is why our text **says "*bin laila haya, u'vin laila avad, In one night it came to be, in one night it perished.*"**

11. **"*Shtayem esrei ribo, a hundred and twenty thousand.*"** Ibn Ezra does not take this number to be the population of Nineveh, or the number of people who had repented for their sins but rather the number of people **who had not sinned,** young children; **also** there are in the city innocent **animals.** These two categories of beings, young children and animals, could not be expected to have moral judgment yet they would have been destroyed with the rest of the city. **For this is the way** we must **reason** understanding that **its destruction would have been** complete, **like the destruction of Sodom,** destroying every living thing. **And this matter is known in all the world.**

3 David Kimchi

Introduction to the Commentary of David Kimchi

Rabbi David Kimchi (1160–1235) is known by the Hebrew acronym, Ra-DaK. He was born in Narbonne, which is in the southeastern corner of what is now France. During Kimchi's life the Catalan dynasty of Barcelona ruled this area, called Provence. The Kimchi family came to Christian Narbonne from the Muslim-controlled portion of Spain, fleeing the fundamentalist Almohades dynasty. The rise of the Almohadeans also caused Abraham Ibn Ezra to leave Spain for Italy.

David Kimchi was part of a scholarly family. His father, Rabbi Joseph Kimchi, and his brother, Rabbi Moses Kimchi, were both noted Bible commentators. He quotes his father in his commentary to the book of Jonah.

In addition to Bible commentary, David Kimchi was a major figure in the study of Hebrew grammar. He wrote Michlol, an early comprehensive study of Hebrew grammar.

I find the commentary of David Kimchi to be clear and readable. His comments make sense to our contemporary ear. While he uses traditional sources, he avoids the more fanciful Midrashim. He often quotes the Targum. He draws upon the commentary of Abraham Ibn Ezra.

At times, rather than giving "the" answer to questions raised by an unclear text, he provides alternative choices without indicating which one he favors.

One could describe Kimchi's commentary as psychological. He examines Jonah's inner process. He tells us what Jonah must have been thinking during the events described in the text. We will see this particularly in chapter two as Jonah prays from the belly of the big fish. Kimchi provides what might be described as Jonah's "voice over."

We will see Kimchi's interest in Hebrew grammar in his Jonah commentary. He pays particular attention to vowels of verbs. He precisely sorts out the verb forms. While we take Hebrew grammar as a given, in the Middle Ages it was still a new field of study. David Kimchi was a pioneer in the area.

Kimchi explains that the Bibles uses metaphors in describing God. It speaks of God in human terms so that we will understand it.

While he comments on the vast majority of the verses in the book of Jonah, Kimchi does on occasion say that the meaning of this verse "is clear" and therefore does not require a comment.

In Pirke Avot 3:17 Rabbi Eliezer ben Azariah teaches, *"Ein kemach ein Torah*, where there is no flour there is no Torah," meaning when people do not have food to eat they cannot study. Students of Rabbi David Kimchi adapted this text to say, *"Ein Kimchi ein Torah*, when there is no Kimchi there is no Torah."

Rabbi David Kimchi's Commentary on Jonah

Chapter One

1. *"Vayahi davar YHVH El Yonah ben Amittai laymor, And the word of The Eternal came to Jonah the son of Amittai saying."* This is the prophet, from whom **we did not see prophecy written by him except for that which he prophesied concerning Nineveh. But we did find** a reference to **prophecy by him** elsewhere in the Bible **but** the words of that prophecy **were not recorded. As it is written in the book of Kings, "It was he**, King Jeroboam son of Joash, **who restored the territory of Israel from Levo-Hamat to the sea of the Aravah, in accordance with the promise of the Lord, the God of Israel, that was spoken through His servant, the prophet Jonah son of Amittai from Gat-Hepher"** (2 Kgs 14:25). **And there is concerning this matter,** of how many times God spoke to Jonah, **a disagreement in the writings of our sages, of blessed memory** (BT Yevamot 98a).

Kimchi turns to another subject before exploring the disagreement of the sages concerning the 2 Kings passage and the number of times God spoke to Jonah. **They,** the authors of the Mechilta, **say, "Jonah seeks the honor of the son and does not seek the honor of the father."** Kimchi wants to clarify the meaning of the words "seeks the honor" from the Mechilta. **They mean to say he fears for the honor of Israel, therefore** he flees to outside the Land of Israel **that is not a place of prophecy so that the God, Who is Blessed, will not** speak to him there to **send him to Nineveh. For he knew that they,** the Ninevites, **were close to repentance and there would be in this punishment for Israel.** If the Ninevites repent in response to one visit from one prophet of the God, God's anger against the Israelite will grow because the Israelites do not repent despite repeated pronouncements from a series of prophets. God's anger would be expressed in punishments for the Israelites. **And he did not fear for the honor of the God, Who is Blessed.**

Kimchi now returns to the disagreement concerning the number of times God spoke to Jonah. **And this is what is said, "And the word of the Eternal came to Jonah a second time"** (3:1). Is this is **the second time He spoke to him not the third?** If the events of 2 Kings had occurred before the events of this story shouldn't the text read "And the word of the Eternal came to Jonah a third time?" **And they raise a difficulty, is it not written, "that was spoken through his servant Jonah ben Amittai the prophet?"** (2 Kgs 14:25). The events described in 2 Kings, God's words here in chapter one of the book of Jonah and those in chapter three would make a total of three times that God spoke to Jonah. Kimchi presents two ways out of this problem from two groups of sages. **And they,** the first sages, **explained it** as follows: **On the matter of Nineveh He spoke to him twice and not three times.** The word "second" in the third chapter of the book of Jonah does not express the total number of times that the Eternal spoke to Jonah, but rather the number of times that the Eternal spoke to Jonah concerning going to Nineveh. **And what do they,** the other sages, **say? He did not speak to him except in regards to Nineveh and not in another matter, rather a second time and not a third.** These sages maintain that the word "second" does indeed refer to the total number of times that the Eternal spoke to Jonah. **And** if that is so **what is meant by "that was spoken through his servant Jonah ben Amittai"?** Those who support this second opinion must explain this phrase from 2 Kings as referring to something other than words of prophecy which God instructed Jonah to speak to Jeroboam ben Joash. **I want to say that this** event in 2 Kings **is similar** to the events in chapter three of the book of Jonah where we read that **they reversed themselves in Nineveh from evil to good. And so it was in the days of Jeroboam ben Joash they reversed themselves from evil to good.** The argument is that the second half of the 2 Kings verse is not referring to words spoken at the time of the events being described but rather offers an analogy. The borders of Israel in the time of Jeroboam ben Joash were restored by God in response to the repentance of the people of Israel just as the city of Nineveh had been spared because the Ninevites had responded to the message of Jonah. This interpretation maintains the total number of times that God spoke to Jonah as two.

And this prophet, Jonah, **was from the tribe of Zebulun. From the appearance that Gat-Hepher was the name of his city. And it is in the portion** of the Land of Israel **of Zebulun as it is written** in Joshua's division of the Land of Israel, "The third lot emerged for the Zebulunites . . . **to Gat-hepher, to Et-Kazin"** (Josh 19:10, 13).

And it could be asked why is this prophecy written in the Holy Scriptures? For it is entirely about Nineveh which is one of the gentile **nations of the world? And there is no mention of Israel here! And there is nothing else in the** books of the **prophets like it. We are able to explain that it was written to be a moral lesson to Israel. Behold a foreign nation that is not a part of Israel was close to repentance and the first time that a prophet rebuked them they turned to a complete repentance from evil. And** what about **Israel,** whom **the prophets rebuke from dawn until dark, and** still **they do not turn from their evil?**

Kimchi presents two other explanations for the inclusion of this story in our sacred literature. **And also to make known to Nineveh the great wonder which the God, Who is Blessed performed, that** Jonah **was in the belly of the fish for three days and three nights and lived. And also to teach that the God, Who is Blessed, is merciful to those who repent from any nation and grants them mercy even more so when they are many** in number. The last verse of the book of Jonah (4:11) tells that Nineveh contains 120,000 people.

2. "*Ukra aleha ki altah ra'atam lifanai, Proclaim upon it for its evil has arisen in my eyes.*" **It is not written** here in chapter one, **what he will proclaim over her. But from what he does proclaim in the end, "Nineveh will be overturned"**(3:4) **we learned that this is the proclamation that He said to him** here in chapter one **to proclaim over her.**

The text of God's call to Jonah, here in chapter one, does not include the words which God wants Jonah to proclaim over Nineveh. One might assume that God does not tell Jonah what to say until later in the story. Based on this way of reading the text we would conclude that Jonah flees from the very idea of a mission to Nineveh without knowing what God wants him to proclaim there. Kimchi reads the text differently contending that the words, which Jonah eventually speaks in Nineveh, were part of

God's initial call to Jonah. Therefore, Jonah flees because he knows exactly what he will have to proclaim in Nineveh.

"Ki alta ra'atam lifanai, For its evil has arisen in my eyes." We can **learn** from this verse **that the God, Who is Blessed, takes note of** sins of **the nations of the world when their evil grows in** *chamas*, **violence.** Kimchi uses the word *chamas* to describe the sins of the Ninevites. The Torah uses *chamas* to describe the evil of the generation of Noah and of the people of Sodom. In both of these cases God takes note of the sins of non-Israelites and punishes them by wiping them out. **And so it is in generation of Noah and in the people of Sodom. And the violence destroys the community. And God, Who is Blessed, is concerned about all the communities in the world. But the rest of their sins are not so important before Him that He would take note of them, rather** He does so **only for Israel.** God becomes concerned about the sins of the other nations when they rise in severity and cross the Chamas threshold. But God holds the Israelites to a higher standard. God is concerned about all the sins of the Israelites. To support this view Kimchi presents a biblical proof text. **As it says, "Only you do I know from all the families of the earth** that is why I hold you to account for all your sins" **As is explain in the prophecies of Amos** (3:2).

3. *"Vayakom Yonah livroach Tarshishah milifnei YHVH, And Jonah arose to flee towards Tarshish from before The Eternal."* **How would he be able to flee?** Kimchi begins his comment with a citation from Psalms that seems to describe the same situation which we find here in Jonah. For King **David says, "How can I flee, *mipanecha*, from your presence?"** (Ps 139:7). Now Kimchi points out that two verses use similar but not identical words to describe a departure from God's presence. We should not be distracted by the difference in the ending of the two words. The words end differently because the word in Jonah is in the third person while the word in Psalms is in the second person. The key difference is that the word in Jonah has a Lamed that does not appear in the word in Psalms. **Rather *milifnei* is not like *mipnei*. For the prophet,** Jonah, **was filled with wisdom and knowledge** for he was receiving prophecy. **And was he thinking to flee *mipnei* from the Eternal?** No, **rather he is thinking to flee *milifnei*, from before the Eternal. For the explanation of *milifnei* speaks of being *lifnei*, before, the Eternal. And that is the spirit of prophecy. For he thought that if he left the Land of Israel to** a place **outside the Land** of Israel **the spirit of prophecy would not rest on him.** Kimchi understands that following the Psalms verse no one can flee from God's presence. Since no matter where

we are, we stand in God's Presence. However, one can attempt to flee from before the spirit of prophecy of God, which is only present in the Land of Israel.

And when he was summoned to go on this mission for Jonah said to himself, **the gentiles are close to repentance and if I go on this mission the God, Who is Praised, will turn them from their evil paths. And Israel will be accused by this** action. **For I, and other prophets, constantly come to them on a mission from the God, Who is Blessed, and they do not turn from their evil path. Therefore he did not accept this mission. Thus is the explanation of the sages of blessed memory** in the Mechilta to Parshat Bo. **Because of this it was impossible** for him to accept his mission. **So he said** to himself **the Shechinah, the presence of God** from which prophecy flows, **does not function outside the Land** of Israel. **And since the gentiles are close to repentance and he did not want to obligate Israel** to punishment for being unwilling to repent **therefore he fled. And the Holy One of Praise said to him, "I have others like you."** God does not mean, "I have other prophets like you to send to Nineveh." In fact one of the key points of the story is that God does not turn to another prophet after Jonah flees. Here God explains, "I have other messengers, including the elements of nature, at my disposal." **And the Eternal sent a great wind to the sea.**

And Rabbi Berechyah ben Yitzhak Halevi points out foolishness of Jonah's attempting to escape by the sea. Rabbi Berechyah **said, "Generally when a man seeks to flee and he flees to a place where he can stand** safely out of the reach of the person from whom he is fleeing. Here **you have a man who flees to one who is** also **in flight** from God. For **the sea flees. As it says, 'The sea saw and ran away'** (Ps 114:3). The sea itself flees before the presence of God, **And you** foolishly **fled to the sea."**

And Targum Yonatan explains the phrase *milefnei Adonai* as meaning "**before he prophesied in the name of the Eternal.**" The Targum presents a different understanding of the word pair *milifnei Adonai*. The other sources see these words referring to space, the Targum sees them as referring to time. The other sources understand the phrase "from before the presence of God" as describing Jonah leaving the place where God was speaking to him. The Targum understands the "from before the presence of God" as describing a time before which he received the word's of God's prophecy.

"*Vayeired Yaffo, And he descended to Jaffa.*" Jonah could have gone down to Jaffa **from his city which was Gat Heffer or from Jerusalem.** In either case he would be starting in the mountains. **And he went down to Jaffa which was on the shore of the sea. And it is a ship harbor. And those who enter the sea are described as "those who go down."** As it says "They go down to the sea in ships" (Ps 107:23). **For the shore of the sea is a low area,** its elevation is at sea level **as compared to the rest of the dry land. My father, of blessed memory,** Rabbi Joseph Kimchi, **said that the explanation of why the word "going down" is used in connection with ships is that the ship is deep and one goes down into it. As it says "He found a ship . . . and went down into it"** (1:3). **And therefore it says "Jonah went down into the hold of the ship"** (1:5). **And thus** the verse from Psalms says, **"They go down to the sea in ships."**

"*Vayimtza oniya ba'a Tarshish, And he found a ship going Tarshish.*" The problem is that the text does not clearly say that Jonah found a ship going <u>to</u> Tarshish. There is no preposition Lamed, to, preceding the word *Tarsheesh*. The verb *ba'a* could be a past tense form indicating the ship had come from Tarshish or it could be a participle indicating the ship was on its way to Tarshish. The word *ba'a* **has its accent on the first syllable** identifying it as a participle **and it means to say that** the ship **was designated to go** back and forth **to and from Tarshish.**

"*Vayitein s'charah, And he paid its fare.*" Kimchi offers three explanations of how Jonah knew how much to pay and that he should pay as he boarded the ship:

1. **The payment that he saw as appropriate to give to** the agent collecting money.

2. **He,** the agent, **told him,** Jonah, **to give** him the money.

3. All the passengers followed the custom and **gave it,** the payment, **at the beginning** of the voyage. And Jonah paid the same amount the other passengers paid.

Kimchi now turns his attention another question concerning the suffix of the word, s'char<u>ah</u>, its fare. Why does the text say "its fare" rather than the fare for a seat or a person. The use of "its fare" suggests that he paid the entire cost of all the passenger spaces on the ship. **In the Midrash** (T.B. Nedarim 38a) the text says **that he paid for the entire ship because he was in a hurry to go. And he did not consider** waiting for the ship to fill with **businessmen and women because he was in a hurry to leave. From this it can be derived that prophecy falls only on a rich man** who could afford to cover the costs of such a voyage.

4. "*Chashva l'hishaveir, The ship thought to break apart.*" Clearly a ship does not think. Kimchi explains that this is a poetic image. **This is in the manner of a broad use of the language. It means to say that the men of the ship thought that the ship would break apart.**

5. "*Vayiru hamelachim, And the sailors feared.*" From the context of the verse we can conclude, without doubt, that *hamelachim* refers to the crew of the ship. Some sources see it as derived from *melach,* salt. The sailors are then "salts." Kimchi says that *hamelachim* refers to **those who held the oars.**

"*El yarkitei has'fina, Into the holds of the ship.*" The problem is that Jonah can only have been in one of the holds of the ship. We would expect the text to use the singular form *yarkat,* rather than the plural form, *yarkitai.* It means **one of the holds of the ship.** The use of a plural form when a singular meaning is intended can be found in other places in the Bible. **This is similar to "He was buried in the cities of Gilead"** (Judg 12:7). This verse describes the burial of Jepthah. Even though the text uses the plural "cities" we know that it means he was buried in one of the cities of Gilead. **It is also similar to "On a donkey the son of she-asses"** (Zech 9:9). In this verse the prophet describes the entrance of the future king into Jerusalem riding a donkey. While the verse use a plural form to describe the mother of the donkey, clearly this donkey will have only one mother.

6. "*Vayikrav eilav rav hachoveil, And the captain of the ship drew close to him.*" Kimchi in this comment addresses three issues; the meaning of the word *rav,* why the word *hachoveil* is used to refer to the sailors, and why the word *hachoveil* is in the singular form when it refers to the sailors. *Rav* is **the great one,** the captain, the great one, **among the sailors.** The word *hachoveil* is used to refer to the sailors **because sailors are called *chovlim* for they tighten and loosen *chevlai,* the ropes, of the mast according to their wisdom.** And the singular form *choveil* is used **because it is the general term for the group of sailors. And so it is in Targum Yonaton** where he is called *Rav S'fanaya,* **the captain of the boatmen. And it is a noun in a category of words and the other** examples of words in this category **we have raised** earlier in this commentary on other books of the Bible. **And also it,** *choveil,* **will be a general name for sailors and he is the most prominent** among them. **He guides the ship. According to this words the sailors hold and loosen the ropes.**

"Yitahsait" The captain calls on Jonah to pray to his God as the other people on the ship are praying to their gods. "Perhaps **He will be willing to help us.**" This word in the text is quite unusual, Kimchi looks for other related words elsewhere in the Bible to shed light on its meaning here. **And thus** we find a word with the same root (Eiyen, Shin, Taf) in the book of Psalms: "*Ivdu ashtinotav,* **his plans perish**" (Ps 146:4). **His thoughts will** turn to us and He will decide not to destroy the ship.

And thus in the Aramaic section of the book of Daniel we find another use of this root. **"And the King** *asit,* **considered setting him over** the entire kingdom" (Dan 6:4). The captain says to Jonah, "Pray to your God perhaps He will <u>consider</u> our situation and save us."

It means to say "thought." The captain says to Jonah, "Pray to your God, perhaps His <u>thought</u> will turn to us and save us."

And Targum Yonaton renders it *yitracheim,* **will have mercy.** The captain says to Jonah, "Pray to your God perhaps He will <u>have mercy</u> on us and save us."

7. **"***Ľchu v'napila goralot, Let us cast lots.***" There is something puzzling in this matter. Why did they think that on account of the men of this ship the Eternal sent this big storm to the sea? Were not there other ships in the sea? And do the crews of all ships that are in a storm at sea cast lots to learn on whose the evil** be fallen them? **I found in Pirkai D'Rebbe Eliezer** (chapter ten) an explanation of how this storm in the book of Jonah was different from the storms that sailors regularly encounter. **"A great storm came upon them in the sea.** But **to their right and to their left all** the other **ships were passing back and forth in peace and quiet. And the ship which Jonah had boarded was in great difficulty, that 'was about to break up.' They said, 'On whose account has this evil befallen us?'** So that **we will know on whose account this evil has be fallen us,** we will cast lots **for the sake of** learning **who he is."**

8. **"***Vayomru, And they said.***"** In the verse the sailors ask Jonah a series of questions without waiting for him to respond between the questions. Kimchi separates the questions to explain the reasons for the individual inquiries.

"Hagida na lanu ba'asher ľmi hara'ah, Please tell us on whose account is this evil?" Now that we know **that you are he on whose account this evil has be fallen us** answer the following questions for us, so that we will understand the reason for this storm.

"Mah melatecha, What is your work?" **For what sin are you sought? What was your work? Perhaps it was the work of swindling and violence and because of this you are obligated,** deserving punishment.

"Umay'aiyin tavo, From where have you come?" **Perhaps you fled from some evil you did there.**

"Mah artzecha, What is your land?" **Perhaps the sons of that land are the sons of evil people.**

"V'ai-mizeh am ata, And from what people are you?" This final question is asked in a peculiar manner. We would have expected the text to use *mayaizeh*, instead in uses *ai-mizeh*. Kimchi provides us with two ways of understanding this choice of words. **One could reason it was used as if it,** the sequence of the first two words of this phrase **was reversed,** *may'aizeh* rather than *ai-mizeh*. **As if he said "From what people are you?" Or it could be explained without reversing** the sequence of the words. **"This people that you are from, what** type **of people is it? A people who have turned away from the God of Blessing by the evil of their deeds?"**

9. *"Vayomeir, And he said."* Jonah does not answer all of the sailors' questions. **On two subjects he gives them answers. When he says to them,** *"Ivri anochi, I am a Hebrew,"* **they know his people and his land. When he says to them,** *"v'et YHVH Elohei hashamayim ani yarei, The Eternal, the God of heaven I fear,"* **he responds to their question, "What is your work?" For his work is not the work of deceit but rather** is an expression of the fact that **he fears the Eternal. And he does not do injustice.**

Why as part of his reply to the sailors' question does he describe God by **saying,** *"Asher-asa et-hayam v'et-hatabasha, Who made the sea and created the dry land"*? **Since they were engulfed by a storm at sea, he said the God, Who is Blessed, made the sea. And He sent the storm wind upon it. And He will quiet it when He will want to, and deliver us to dry land. And he says that "of the heavens" He is God, for He directs them and causes them to flow. And** why does he not say **he says "of the earth that He made"?** The explanation for this omission is found in the word **"completed." For the earth was not created from the beginning, completed to meet the needs of living creatures.** The earth could not sustain these creatures **until** after **the concentration of the waters** into seas on the third day of creation. The heavens and the seas were completed at the moment of their creation but not the earth. This is why Jonah does not speak here "of the earth He made."

10. **"Vayiru, They feared."** The verse concludes, *"for he told them."* This phrase raises two questions: What did he tell them? When did he tell it to them? Kimchi explains Jonah's declaration of his identity recorded in verse nine was part of a fuller conversation which is not included in the text. **For he told them when he said** in verse 9, **"The Eternal, the God of the heavens I fear."** Kimchi reconstructs the rest of the conversation. **They said to him, "If that is the case why is this storm here on your account?" He said to them, "I am a prophet and the God, Who is Blessed, sent me to Nineveh. And** going to Nineveh **was difficult in my eyes so I came to you. I fled from before** God. **And I went out of the land of Israel for that is the place of prophecy."**

11. **"Ki hayam holaich v'soeir, For the sea was going and storming."** The sailors ask Jonah what can they do to appease God. Kimchi imagines them saying, **"For we have no hope that the sea will become quiet** without God's intervention **because the storm increases in ferocity."**

   "Vayeshtok hayam, To quiet the sea." The sailors want to know what they can do to convince God to quiet the sea in this **place of its strong waves.** Kimchi refers to the Psalm which describes "they who go down to the sea in ships" seeing God's power expressed in the "wonders of the deep." The Psalm describes a storm with huge waves. The sailors caught in that storm cry out to God who responds to their prayer. **As it says,** "He made the storm a calm, so that its waves were still. **They** (the sailors) **rejoiced for they** (the waves) **were quiet"** (Ps 107:29–30)

12. **"V'sheli, And mine."** On my account, that is to say, because of the sin that is mine.

13. **"Vayach't'ru, They dug."** This verb usually is used to describe digging. Kimchi explains its use here to describe rowing. **They pulled on the oars strongly to bring the ship to dry land. For they held on to the oars and placed them in the sea like shovels.**

   And Targum Yonaton renders the word in Aramaic as **v'shayatin,** they rowed.

   And why does the text say *"l'hashiv, to return"* to the dry land? It could simply have said that they rowed "toward" the shore. **It is because it was from the dry land that the ship departed and when the ship would leave the sea for the dry land, it,** the ship, **would be returning to it, the** dry land.

14. *"Vayikr'u, And they called."* The meaning of the opening phrase of the verse **is clear** and does not require explanation.

"Ana, Please." The prayer is directed to the **He who is God.**

"Naki, Clean." This is an unusual spelling of this word. We would have expected to find it spelled Nun, Koof, Yud. But here in our text there is an Alef at the end of the word. **It is written with an Alef like other words which** have Yud as their third letter and **end in Alef, like *naki* and *nasi.***

15. *"Vayis'u, And they lifted."* The meaning of this verse **is clear** and does not require explanation.

16. *"Vayizb'chu Zevach, They offered an offering."* The text does not clearly define the time and place of this offering. **They did not offer the offering on the ship. Rather its explanation is according to the Targum, "And they said they will offer offerings before the Eternal."** That is at the Temple in Jerusalem after their return to the land.

"Vayidru Nedarim, "They vowed vows." One might think that these oaths refer to the sailors' intention to bring a sacrifice to the Temple in Jerusalem. Kimchi explains that this promise refers to **other oaths beyond their pledge to offer an offering such as giving *tzedaka* to poor people.**

Chapter Two

1. *"Vay'man YHVH, And The Eternal designated."* At first reading it seems to an odd choice for this context. The verse could have said God directed the big fish or God commanded the big fish. To explain the use of this word Kimchi finds another place in the Bible that uses this root in a manner similar to its use here in our verse. In the book of Daniel it is used to describe food that had been designated for Daniel to eat. **This is a matter of assignment. It is similar to "who allotted to you food"** (Dan 1:10). The king assigned specific food to Daniel and the other selected youths of Judah. **And the God of Blessing assigned him,** the fish, this task **for a specific time. At the** exact **time that Jonah was thrown into the sea the fish was assigned** to be in the right spot **to swallow him.** And this fish is not **naturally in this sea. And this was one of the miracles. And in Pirkai D'Rabbi Eliezer Rabbi Tarfon says, "The fish was appointed from the sixth day of creation to swallow Jonah."** The sages taught that wonders such as the big fish that occurred in the Bible were not contrary to nature but rather were built into the world as part of the act of creation. The sages

suggest that these wonders, such as the dividing of the sea by Moses or the sun standing still in the sky for Joshua, were incorporated into creation by God on the afternoon of the sixth day (see Genesis Rabbah 5:5 and Berachot 8a).

2. **"*Vayitpalail Yonah, And Jonah prayed.*" It was a great miracle that he was in the belly of the fish three days and three nights and remained alive. It is another miracle that he was not in shock but rather could remain in control of his knowledge and his thoughts and** be able to **pray.**

"*Hadaga, The fish.*" In verse 1 the word used for the fish is *dag*, the masculine form. Here in verse 2 we find *daga*, the feminine form. **This is similar to *dag*,** in verse 1. This word **appears** in the Bible **in the masculine and in the feminine for example, "And the *daga*, fish, that are in the Nile will die"** (Exod 7:18). This verse is from the description of what will take place during the first plague. The word *daga*, here in the feminine form, clearly refers to all fish. The text should certainly not be understood to say that when the Nile is turned into blood the feminine fish will die but the masculine fish will survive.

There is an interpretation found in Rashi's commentary **that it was a feminine fish** in verse 2 and a masculine fish in verse one, **according to the teachings of the sages.**

One could reason that "*mim'ei*" is not a place. Most commentators understand "*mim'ei*" to refer to a specific place, "from the belly" of the fish, **as it is rendered in Targum Yonaton. Rather I want to say** it describes Jonah's state of mind, **from the midst of difficulty he prayed. And thus** in the next verse we read **"From the *beten*, belly, of Sheol I cried out"** (2:3), which is similar to **"From the depths I called unto you Eternal One"** (Ps 130:1) and **"In distress I called upon the Lord"** (Ps 118:5). In each case "from" expresses state of mind rather than location.

3. "*Vaya'aneini, And He answered me.*" We would expect that Jonah would not use the past tense until he was entirely out of danger. **Even though he stood in His creature he knew that he would exit the belly of the fish in peace.**

4. "*Nahar y'sov'veini, The river spun around me.*" **The river that entered the sea. And the wise Rabbi Abraham Ibn Ezra explained that this was the place where the sea and the river mixed.**

"Kol mishbarecha v'galecha, All Your breakers and Your waves." In the breaking of the waves of the sea at the moment they billow they are called *mishbarei,* **breakers.**

5. *"Va'ani amarti nigrashti, And I said, 'I was driven* from your sight.'" Why is the verb in a passive voice? Jonah was not driven away from God, he fled. **I thought that when they threw me into the sea I was dead.** Therefore I would have no further contact with You, I was driven from your presence by the act of the sailors.

"V'nigrashti mineged einecha, I was driven from your sight." **That is to say from when you kept watch over me,** when I served as a prophet, **until I thought that You hid Your face and eyes from me** during my flight. **But now that You have performed this great miracle for me and I continue to be alive here in the belly of the fish I thought that I will again be able to gaze upon your dwelling place of your holiness in the Temple and the place of prophecy and the place where you will watch over me. Cause me to return to it because I fled from it.**

And the explanation of *"l'habit, to gaze at Your Holy Temple,"* **is** that Jonah hopes **to** again **pray at the Temple** in Jerusalem.

6. *"Afafuni mayim ad-nefesh, The waters encompassed me to my soul."* Kimchi explains the poetic image and provides a similar use of this image from the book of Psalms. **The water swirled around me until my soul was about to depart and then the fish swallowed me. And similarly "Until the waters have come unto my soul"** (Ps 69:2). The speaker in the Psalm also describes feeling the threat of imminent death.

"Suf chavush l'roshi, suf wrapped around my head." Suf **is the reed. There is a type** of reed **which grows on the banks of the Nile and shores of the sea. Therefore the reeds which grow on the shores and banks are called** *suf rav,* **great reeds. And there is a type** of reeds **which grows on floor of the sea at the base of the mountains. And it is called algae in French. It is thin and long and it wraps around the heads of fish. And that is what happens here when it says** *"suf chavush l'roshi, The reeds wrapped around my head."*

The explanation of *"roshi, my head,"* **is "the head of the fish that swallowed me." For his** head, Jonah's **was like his,** the fish's **head all the time that he was in the fish. And there are those who explain** *suf* **as the Sea of Reeds. They say that the Sea of Reeds enters into the Sea of Yaffo on this path. And Targum Yonaton renders it, "The Sea of Reeds hangs over from** above **my head."**

7. **"L'kitzei harim yaraditi, To the ends of the mountains I descended." To the end of the mountains that are in the sea. That is to say to their roots that are at the floor of the sea in its extreme depth. And Targum Yonaton renders it "I went down to the foundation of the mountains."**

"Ha'aretz b'richeha va'adi l'olam, The land its bars against me forever." Kimchi imagines Jonah's thoughts. **"From the beginning I thought that the land, the dry land, its bars against me that is to say** the way to reach dry land **was barred against me.** I feared **that I would never be able to go up** to dry land. **And the sea would be my grave. And after I was alive in the belly of the fish I knew that I would escape from this pit alive and the pit would not be my grave but rather I would return to dry land."**

"YHVH Elohai, The Eternal, my God." **That you have ruled on my cases with justice.** The use of the four letter name of God suggests God's attribute of justice as opposed to the use of the name Elohim which would indicate God's attribute of mercy at work.

Kimchi returns to his consideration of the phrase, *"ha'aretz b'richeha va'adi."* **And Targum Yonaton renders it, "The land strong against me . . ."**

8. *"B'hitateif alai nafshi, In the wrapping upon me of my soul."* The first word is this phrase describes "wrapping". It may be familiar from the blessing for putting on one's tallit (prayer shawl). Kimchi explains its use here to describe a soul about to faint. **This is the language that speaks about most of the suffering that shortens the soul,** the life, **of a person and thus their soul are wrapped up in it.** Jonah **says when my soul was afflicted,** when my life was threatened, **when the fish swallowed me immediately I thought I would die. Even so I remembered the God of Blessing and prayed to him.**

"V'tavo eilecha t'philati, And my prayer came to you." **Since I remained alive in the belly of the fish I knew that my prayer would come to you.** Jonah concludes that God is paying attention to him from the miraculous manner in which a fish saved him from drowning. Therefore he can be confident that his prayer will indeed come before God.

"El Heichal kadshecha, To the Temple of Your holiness." This is the heavens and for it says, "The Eternal is in his holy palace, His throne in the heavens" (Ps 11:4) and in this manner, "Their prayer went up to his holy abode, to heaven" (2 Chr 30:27). Kimchi brings these verses to counter the notion that the text may be referring to the Temple in Jerusalem. Kimchi reject the image of the Temple as God's abode.

9. *"M'shamrim chevlei shav, They devotedly serve vanities of worthlessness."* The men of the ship worshiped many gods, they *"devotedly serve vanities of worthlessness."* Kimchi explains the use of the word "guarded" to indicate that the sailors maintained their beliefs in false gods even after the events described here. Kimchi imagines Jonah reflecting, **"I knew that after they were saved from their difficulty they would depart from their kindness, from their fear of the Eternal to whom they had cried out and sworn vows. They did not fulfill their vows but rather returned to their worship of many gods. But I did not act like that. Rather in a voice of thanks I worshipped You."**

"M'shamrim, Guard." **This is not a transitive verb,** as Ibn Ezra contends, **rather it is like** *shomrim,* **guards.**

There is a Midrash concerning *"chasdam ya'azovu, their righteousness departed."* **From this** false **righteousness** they departed. **That is to say they departed from their** worship of **false gods which had been their** former mistaken **righteousness.** Now they had come realize it was **vile.**

And thus in Pirkai D'Rebbe Eliezer, since the sailors when they arrived in Nineveh "saw all the miracles that The Holy One of Praise did with Jonah, they stood up and each man cast away his god into the sea. As it says, *"Those who devotedly serve vanities of worthlessness, they will forsake their righteousness."* And they returned to Yaffo and went up to Jerusalem and circumcised the flesh of their foreskins. As it says *"The men feared The Eternal greatly and they offered offerings"* (1:16). The offering of offerings is the blood of the covenant of circumcision for it is like the blood of an offering. And each man vowed to bring his wife and children and everything he had to the fear of The Eternal, the God of Jonah. And they made vows and fulfilled them. And concerning them it says in the Amidah, "For the proselytes, the proselytes of righteousness."

Targum Yonaton renders it, "Not like gentile worshippers was their error . . ."

10. *"Va'ani b'kol todah, And I with a voice of thanksgiving."* Kimchi explains the two parts of the verse as referring to two types of thanksgiving, public and communal on one hand, and private and individual on the other. **That I will thank you with a voice of thanksgiving from the midst of the congregation.** As is written in the second part of the verse *"Ezbcha-lach asher nidarti, And I will offer thanksgiving offerings as I have vowed."*

And the explanation of the fact that **that he says "*Y'shuata laYHVH, Salvation is the Eternal's*," privately, is that** Jonah understands, "God saved me through a wonder He performed for me."

11. "*Vayomeir YHVH ladag, The Eternal spoke to the fish.*" God did not literally have a conversation with the fish. But rather **He revealed His will** to the fish **so that it would spit him on to dry land.**

Chapter Three

1. "*Vayahee davar YHVH el Yonah shaynit, And the word of The Eternal came to Jonah a second time.*" **We have already explained the meaning of "second"** in the comment to the first verse of the first chapter.

2. "*Kum, Arise.*" It is as if God says to Jonah, "**For I tell to you now what I told you before. Now also I will tell you what you will proclaim, 'That it,** Nineveh, **will be overturned because of its sins.'"** In God's call to Jonah in chapter one the content of the proclamation is not described.

3. "'*Ir g'dola Lailohim, A great city to God.*" The issue here is why in describing the size of Nineveh does the text say *Lailohim,* to God? Kimchi explains that **everything the Bible wants to enlarge** through description **it connects it to God in order to enlarge it. This is similar to** other biblical examples of descriptions which connect places or events to God in order to intensify the image. In each case the quoted phrase contains a reference to God that is understood to increase the description rather than to invoke the Deity. Therefore the literal reference to God does not appear in the translations. "*Kahar'rei eil, The high mountains*" (Ps 36:7), "*arzei eil, mighty cedars*" (Ps 80:11), "*aish shavhevet'yah, a blazing flame,*" (Song of Songs 8:6), **and** "*mapeil yah,*" *Deep darkness*" (Jer 2:31).

4. "*Vayachel Yonah, And Jonah started.*" **For the city was a three day's walk from end to end and Jonah began to enter the city the distance of a one day's walk. He was proclaiming** as he walked. **And he said, "*Od arba'im yom v'nineveh neh'pachet, In forty days Nineveh will be overturned.*"** I **want to say that this is similar to the overturning of Sodom and Gomorrah for their deeds,** the deeds of Nineveh, **were like their deeds,** the deeds of Sodom and Gomorrah.

5. *"Vaya'aminu, And they believed."* Why do the Ninevites respond so dramatically to Jonah's words? **For the men of the ship were in the city and they gave testimony concerning him.** They told the story of the storm and **that they threw him into the sea.** They said, **"And all of our witnessing is exactly as it happened." Therefore** the Ninevites **believed in his prophecy and made a complete repentance** for their sins.

"Vayikr'u tzom, And they declared a fast." The question here is which came first, the king's proclamation described in verse six or the people's repentance mentioned here in verse five? The sequence of the verses certainly suggests that the people acted before the king spoke. Some commentators, i.e., Ibn Ezra, argue that the sequence of the verses does not reflect the sequence of events. Kimchi, however, argues that **before the warning of the king, they made repentance on their own. They humbled themselves and put on sackcloth.**

6. *"Vayigah hadavar, And the word reached* the King of Nineveh." Kimchi explains to what word *hadavar* refers. **The word of the prophecy spoke and proclaim on the city.**

"Adarato, His glory." **The robe of royalty he was wearing. And Targum Yonaton renders it "clothing of honor."**

7. *"Vayazaik, And it was proclaimed."* **He caused an announcement be made in the city concerning the repentance. And even though the people were already enlightened concerning God. This added to the contrition of the animals,** they now had to fast also, **and the repentance of the thief,** who would not have been moved to repent by his own conscience.

"Mita'am hamelech ug'dolav, From the Ta'am of the kings and his great ones." I want to **say** this means **from his advice and his wisdom. He and his nobles together agreed on this. And thus the reasoning of the elders accepted in their teaching his reasoning which was similar to their** reasoning. **And Targum Yonaton renders it, "Ruling of the King."**

8. *"B'chazaka, With strength."* **With all** their **hearts.**

"Midarko hara'ah, From his evil way." **From all types of sin.**

"Umin hechamas, And from violence." **This** sin of violence **is equal to all of them,** the other sins. **And for this** sin **the proclamation was issued.** As noted in the explanation of Kimchi's comment to 1:2, the Hebrew Bible uses this word *chamas* to describe the generation of Noah and the population of Sodom. Its use here puts the sins of the Ninevites in the same category of those of the generation of Noah and the people of Sodom.

9. **"*Mi-yodai'ah,* Who knows."** This phrase does not have a clear referent. Kimchi provides two different ways to read the phrase. The first possibility is that the Ninevites are speculating about God's response to their repentance. "<u>Who knows</u>? **Perhaps God will have mercy on us in response to our repentance from our evil deeds.**" The second possibility is that it refers to former sinners among the Ninevites. **Or it could be explained, the one <u>who knows </u>the paths of repentance will repent and the God of Blessing will have mercy.**

And Targum Yonaton renders the verse "Who knows there is here evidence of repentance of the Ninevites **settled correctly and mercy comes upon them from the Eternal."**

"*V'nicham, And* God *will repent.*" **There is a Patach** under the Chet **because this is a past tense verb form with the meaning of referring to the future because the Eternal will cause it,** turning away from the plan to destroy Nineveh, **to happen. And this form is from the Nifal conjugation.**

10. **"*Vayar, And* God *saw.*"** God saw that the Ninevites turned away f**rom their evil path in general,** and **from all the evil and from the violence they made a complete repentance. As our sages said, "He who steals a beam and builds upon it a great building undermines the entire building when he returns the beam to its owner"** (Tosephta Baba Kamma 10:5).

"*Vayinachem Haelohim, And God repented.*" **This is similar to all** God's **pronouncements to evil people on the condition that they do not repent. But if they do repent** God **will forgive. And this** is an expression **of that aspect among the aspects of the One who is Blessed. As it says in the Torah** "Extending kindness to the thousandth generation, forgiving iniquity, transgression and sin" (Exod 34:7). **And thus says Jeremiah, "At one moment I may decree** that a nation or a kingdom shall be uprooted and pulled down and destroyed; but if that nation against which I made the decree turns back from its wickedness, I change my mind concerning the punishment I planned to bring on it" (Jer 18:7–8).

And thus says Ezekiel, the book of Ezekiel contains two verses which begin with the words quoted by Kimchi. Both verses illustrate the point Kimchi is making in his comment, **"And if a wicked man turns back from the wickedness** that he practiced and does what is just and right, such a man shall save his life. Because he took heed and turned back from all the transgressions that he committed, he shall live; he shall not die" (Ezek 18:27–28) or **"And if a man turns back from his wickedness** and does what is just and right, it is he who shall live by virtue of these things" (Ezek 33:19).

Chapter Four

1. "*Vayaira*, **And it was evil** to Jonah a great evil." We have the root Resh, Eiyen, Hei in both a verb and noun form. Kimchi drawing upon other biblical examples of this root in a verb form explains how we should read the phrase. **They caused him evil. This is similar to** another biblical verse which is read literally as **"What he did was evil in the eyes of The Eternal"** but is understood to mean **"What he did was displeasing to The Eternal"** (Gen 38:10). **And** another example read literally **"Will cause evil to the eye of his brother"** but understood to mean **"Shall be too mean to his brother"** (Deut 28:54). **And so it is with all words in this category.**

And this does not follow the teaching of Rabbi Yehuda ben David.

And how does Jonah know that the people will repent and the city will not be destroyed **for the fortieth day has not yet come?** There is a question here of the sequence of events. The text does not say that "Jonah left the city" until 5. Abraham Ibn Ezra understands verse 5 to mean "Jonah had left the city" sometime earlier. He, therefore, takes all the events described in chapter four as following God's relenting from the destruction of Nineveh described in the last verse of chapter three. Kimchi reads the text differently. He reads verse 4 to mean "Jonah left the city." As a result he understands the first four verses of chapter four to describe activity which took place immediately following Jonah's announcement that "In forty days Nineveh will be overthrown" thus while he was still in the city. Therefore Kimchi asks the question above and provides this answer. **The God of Blessing told him in the spirit of prophecy that He would relent from what He had decreed concerning them because they had repented from their evil paths.**

"*Vayichar lo*, **And it grieved him.**" Why is Jonah angry that God forgives the Ninevites? Because it contrast with the Israelites who do not respond to the messages of the prophets. **This is as we have explained,** in the comment to 1:1, **for the sake of Israel who did not turn from its path of evil.**

2. "*Vayitpalail*, **And he prayed.**" And Jonah prayed "*Kach-na et nafshi, Please take my soul*" (4:3). This verse reports an introduction to the prayer which Jonah recites in the next verse, **And he said in the beginning of his prayer, "*Ana YHVH, Please Eternal.*"**

"*Halo-zeh D'vari*, **Is this not my word?**" What I was thinking and what I said in my heart. For the text of chapter one does not record Jonah saying these words out loud. **For I feared that they would repent and You would relent on the evil. And their repentance would cause evil to Israel.**

"Ana, Please." **It is written in the singular.** Jonah prays for himself.

"Ad-heyoti, When I was." **While I <u>still</u> was. And it is similar to "While this one was <u>still</u> speaking"** (Job 1:18).

"Kidamti livroach, I hastened to flee." **Before your prophecy on this matter would come to me a second time.**

"V'nicham, Renouncing." **There is a Kamatz** under the Chet **because this is a present tense verb in the Nifal conjugation** as opposed to a past tense third person masculine singular form, where the vowel would be a Patach. The present tense form of the word indicates that God continues to "renounce" punishing the Ninevites.

3. *"Kach-na et-nafshi, Please take my life."* **So I will not see the evil of Israel.** Jonah does not want to witness suffering befall Israel. **This is similar to Moses our teacher, servant of The Eternal,** when in response to the Israelites building the golden calf he says to God, "If you will not (forgive their sin) then **wipe me out of your book** which you have written" (Exod 32:32). **And it is similar to** Moses' response to the Israelites complaining about the manna, "**Kill me rather,** I beg You, and let me see no more of my wretchedness" (Num 11:15).

4. *"Vayomeir YHVH hahaitaiv charah lach, And The Eternal said, 'Are you greatly grieved?'"* God asks Jonah, **Are you very grieved? And He does not say any more than this.** God **could say that in a little while I will show you a sign that it is not according to the law that you should be grieved concerning my forgiveness to the repentant.**

And the word *haheiteiv* **intensifies the matter described. This** use of *heiteiv* here **is similar to** it use in the description of the destruction of the golden calf. "**I broke it into pieces and ground it <u>completely</u>** until it was fine as dust" (Deut 9:21). Another example of this use of *heiteiv* is found in 2 Kings. "Thereupon all the people of the land went to the Temple of Baal, they tore down its altar and its images **they smashed <u>to bits</u>**" (2 Kings 11:18). **And there are those who,** connect *heiteiv* with *tov,* good. They explain it to mean "**Does the <u>good</u> I do to them grieve you?**" And Targum Yonaton renders it like *halachada*, very.

5. *"Mikedem la'ir, From before the city."* Kimchi explains why Jonah remained in the area. **And he sat in a place that was east of the city. Until**

he would see if perhaps they would not maintain their repentance and God's **verdict would again be in force.**

6. **"Vay'man, And He designated."** He caused it to sprout according to the hour. **For even though he built himself a booth for shade, perhaps the branches of the booth dried out. For he dwelled there until the completion of the forty days.** According to Kimchi, Jonah built the booth on the day of his proclamation that Nineveh would be destroyed in forty days. And then dwelled in it, waiting to see what would happen. **And He made this sign for him to teach him about the Divine decree. For He has mercy on all His creatures.**

"Kikayon" Kimchi provides several possibilities for the identity of this plant. **It is a tall and beautiful plant. Its leaves provide shade. In the Mishnah in TB Shabbat 21a "not with *shemen kik,* the oil of the *kik.* And in the Gemara it is asked, 'What is this *shemen kik?'* Resk Lakish says, 'It is the *kikayon* of Jonah.' Rabbah bar Bar Channah says, "I saw this *kikayon* of Jonah, which is like a *tzuliva."***

And my father, my teacher and my mentor, Rabbi Joseph Kimchi, **explained that it grows between the ditches of water. At the entrances of stores it is grown to provide shade. And from its kernels oil is made.** Kimchi quotes the previous phrase in Aramaic and then provides its translation into Hebrew.

Rabeinu Shmuel ben Hafni says it is a plant that is called in Arabic, Aleveroa.

The explanation of *tzuliva* I found in the responsa of the Gaonim. It is a tree without fruit, which grows in our area in abundance. And it has kernels. And from them oil is made, And everyone who has a cold drinks of it. And its name in Arabic is *alk'rua.*

"Meira'ato, From his discomfort." **From the heat of the sun which struck and dried up the branches of the booth that was his source of shade.**

7. **"Va'aman, And He designated."** This word is used by the text to describe God providing the big fish, the plant, here the worm and in the next verse the wind. God **arranged for the worm to be at the location of the plant at this specific time.**

"Ba'alot hashachar, In the rising of the dawn." **In its house,** that the sun rose to its place in the heavens for that day according to the movement of heavenly bodies.

"Vatach et hakikayon, And it attacked the kikayon." The question here is why does the text use the feminine forms *tola'at* and *vatach* rather than the masculine forms *tola* and *vayach.* **Tola'at, the worm, is a feminine noun.** Kimchi provides another biblical example of this noun in a feminine form accompanied by a feminine verb. **"For the worm will devour them"** (Deut 28:39). The root (Taf, Lamed, Eyin) appears in both masculine and feminine forms to mean worm.

"Vatach, Attacked." **It means to say that** the worm **attacked the lower** part of the plant. **After it stop receiving moisture from the earth it was cut and withered.** The worm did not consume the entire plant. It ate the key part of the plant, causing it to die. **It had been for** a source of **shade. Behold for one day he had this joy and by dawn the next day is was broken and withered.**

8. *"Vay'man, And He designated."* God **arranged for the wind** to blow **at that hour to increase his suffering adding to his suffering from the heat of the sun.**

And the explanation of *charishit,* which might be understood as silent, is that it was **so strong that when it blew that it made people deaf. And Targum Yonaton renders it "Silent"**

An eastern wind is itself hot so that the impact of the sun becomes the impact of the sun and the wind together, the inverse of wind chill.

"Vayitaleif, And it wrapped." **His soul was exhausted and he became quite stricken to the extent that he could no longer stand on his own because of the heat. His spirit was close to departing. He was close to death. This is similar my explanation of** *titalafna* in Amos (8:13). **And this in accord with the words of the sages of blessed memory "Perhaps he will faint."**

9. *"Vayomeir, And He said."* This **verse is very clear.** It requires no explanation.

10. *"Vayomeir YHVH ata chasta al hakikayon, And The Eternal said, 'You pity the Kikayon?'"* **Even though you did not take pity on the plant except because of your suffering, the God of Blessing takes pity on Nineveh because of His glory. For His creatures are His glory. As it is**

written, "The fullness of the earth is His glory" (Isa 6:3). **And the glory of His Name is from man. As it is written, "Whom I created for my glory" (Isa** 43:7). I quote this verse here to refer to the Ninevites **even though we have explained this verse,** in Isaiah, **to refer to Israel. For in every place in which the text speaks about types of people, like it says** in the next part of the Isaiah verse, **"whom I formed and made" it teaches that Israel is valued by God more highly than others as "my treasure." And the sages agree that this verse refers to Israel.**

"Asher lo-ʿamalta bo v'lo gidalta, That you did not work for and you did not grow." **When a person labors for something he will be sadder when it perishes. And even though the God of Blessing did not** actually **labor in the forming of His creations, the Torah speaks in the language of people to bring understanding to the listeners.**

"Shebin-laila haya uvin laila avad, It appeared as the son of a night and perished as the son of a night." First Kimchi explains the unusual word *bin.* **Bin is the same as *ben*, a more common form meaning "son of."**

This word is also used in Hebrew to indicate age. So, for example, *"ben eser,"* which literally means "son of ten," is understood to mean "ten years old". Kimchi provides biblical examples. **Like *"ben chodesh*, one month old"** (Lev 27:6) **or *"ben esrim*, twenty years old"** (Lev 27:5).

Here it is used to express a brief passage of time. **And the explanation of this phrase *"shebeen-laila, The son of a night"* is that in one night the plant sprouted and in the next night it withered at the end of the night. For the text says,** in verse seven in referring to the attack of the worm, **"At the rising of dawn" and it was broken and withered.**

11. *"Harbeih mishtaim-esrei ribo adam, Many than* twelve *myriad of man."* **Which means more than** twelve *myriads* **of people. And a *"Ribo, Myriad"* is ten thousand.**

And the word *"mishtaim,"* despite the lengthening of the word by the addition of the **Mem and** before **the Shin there is no Dagesh** added to it. **The verse uses the word *sh'tayim* and adds the prefix Mem. The Mem is in place of the word *min* (Mem, Nun). So instead of *min shtayim*, we have *mishtaim*.** Often this dropping of the Nun would be accompanied by a Dagesh, a dot, in the Shin to remind the reader of the letter which has been dropped. Kimchi explains that that is not the case here.

"Adam, Man." It **includes males and females.** The reader should not mistaken the number 120,000 to refer to the number of men in Nineveh.

"*Asher lo yada, Who do not know.*" They are children who do not know the difference between their right and their left. And they have no sin and deserve no punishment except on account of their parents. And because the parents repented, the children are without punishment. And so the many animals they had in the city. And the animal deserved no punishment and all of these living creatures, deserve God's concern and protection and even more so because of their number.

4   Isaac Abarbanel

INTRODUCTION TO THE COMMENTARY OF DON ISAAC ABARBANEL

ISAAC ABARBANEL (1437–1508) WAS a financier, an advisor to royalty, a philosopher, and a Bible commentator. He was a prominent leader of the Jewish community of Portugal and Spain during the difficult times of the expulsion of the Jews from those countries.

His approach differs from the earlier commentators in content, structure, and style. He does not delve into the grammar issues explored by Ibn Ezra and Kimchi. Abarbanel focuses on the narrative line of the text.

Moreover, Abarbanel puts forward many new ideas not found in the earlier commentaries. Earlier writers sought to provide a positive motivation for Jonah's flight. Abarbanel goes a step farther by presenting Jonah as a heroic figure prepared to sacrifice himself to save his people. Abarbanel presents a unique understanding of Jonah's prayer in chapter two. He explains that it is in the past tense because it refers not to the difficulties Jonah faces in this story, but rather to a much earlier event in Jonah's life.

Abarbanel provides a new positive explanation for Jonah's despair in chapter four. Most readers see this despair as Jonah's petulant self-centered reaction to God's decision to not destroy Nineveh in response to the repentance of the Ninevites. Abarbanel explains that Jonah was disappointed that God did not hold the Ninevites to a sufficiently high standard. God forgave them even though their repentance was incomplete. They turned from their evil ways, but they remained idol worshippers.

Abarbanel divides the book of Jonah into two sections. At the beginning of each section he lists and explains a series of questions. He then divides his comments as answers to the questions.

Abarbanel explains his ideas fully. He does not depend on his readers to bring as much background or to read as "actively" as do the earlier commentators. He writes in long, complex sentences. He does not begin his comments with words from the verse. He comes to those words during the comment.

Abarbanel draws on rabbinic sources. He refers to Seder Olam. He quotes from Pirke D'Rabbi Eliezer. He refers to Abraham Ibn Ezra as "My Teacher" whether he is agreeing or disagreeing with him. He also refers to David Kimchi's commentary. He also uses astrology to explain the text.

ISAAC ABARBANEL'S COMMENTARY TO THE BOOK OF JONAH

Abarbanel begins his commentary with an introduction. He divides the book of Jonah into two sections according to the two prophecies, the two times God calls Jonah to speak to the Ninevites. **The first prophecy begins** *"Vay'hi d'var YHVH el Yona ben Amittai, And the Eternal spoke to Jonah the son of Amittai."* And it continues **until** the second prophecy *"Vayhi d'var YHVH el Yonah sheinit, And God spoke to Jonah a second time."* (3:1). **And it contains two portions; The first is** *"Vay'hi d'var YHVH el Yona ben Amittai"* (1:1) **and the second is** *"Vayomeir YHVH l'dag, And the Eternal spoke to the fish"* (2:11).

The First Prophecy

It seems to me appropriate to comment on six questions concerning the first prophecy.

The first question: In what Hashem (God; lit. "The Name") **says to Jonah,** *"Kum leich el Nineveh ha'ir hagedola, ukra aleha ki alta ra'atam lifanai, Arise and go to Nineveh, that great city because their evil has arisen before me."* **For what are the people of Nineveh to** God whose **Name is Blessed?** Why does God care **that their misdeeds have increased?** Why does He **pay attention to them to send** one of **His servants, the prophets, to rebuke them and to straighten them out? Is it not known from the beginning that this** prophecy **is the uplifting advantage which The Holy**

One of Blessing provides to His people and His inheritance, the People Israel, **to watch over them in the particular and in general, in a high and wondrous oversight as it says, "The Eternal alone guided them,"** (Deut 32:12) **"For the Eternal's portion is His people, Jacob is the measure of His inheritance"** (Deut 32:9). **In truth the other nations are under the governance of the angels, as the Eternal apportioned to all the nations. And thus for the nation of Israel** alone **are the prophets. They are an instrument of Hashem. And He sends them to rebuke and straighten out** the Israelites. **He does not do so to every nation. What did** the God of **Blessing see to cause Him to send Jonah to Nineveh, the city of the Chaldeans? He did not** send prophets **to Egypt, or to Babylon and the other mighty nations in which their population did evil and sinned greatly before the Eternal.**

The second question: What did Jonah see that caused him **to flee from before Hashem?** Why did he believe that he could flee God? Did he not know that God rules the entire world? **As is written in the Mechilta, for from before Hashem he fled. Has it not already been said, "Where can I go from your spirit, where can I flee from your presence?"** (Ps 139:7). **And it is written, "The eyes of the Eternal which range over all the earth"** (Zech 4:10). **Our sages of blessed memory have already given us two explanations for this matter** of Jonah's flight.

The first explanation: **The nations of the world were close to repentance and he did not want to accuse Israel,** which never repents despite repeated calls from many prophets. **This is a very weak explanation. For perhaps in the repentance of the people of Nineveh the Israelites would be shamed. And they would repent from their sins turning to The Eternal who would have mercy on them for their personal acts** of repentance. This is a **Kal V'Chomer** argument, a traditional rabbinic rule of logic. Literally, "simple and severe" i.e., If I care the children do not go hungry, I certainly care that my own children do not go hungry. **From the gentiles who are not Israelites.** If the Ninevites, who do not have a direct relationship with The Eternal repent in response to Jonah's single proclamation, should not also the Israelites, who do have a close, direct relationship to The Eternal repent in response to the calls of the numerous prophets which the Eternal has sent them?

The second explanation: **They say that Jonah feared that as the people of Nineveh would repent** from their sins **The Eternal would repent from His anger and forgive them. And the people of Nineveh would say**

that Jonah lied and that he is a false prophet. This also does not make sense to me. **For the people of Nineveh believed in** the words of **Jonah and therefore performed repentance growing out of** the words of **his mouth. And he knew that if they returned in repentance as a result of his words they** must of **had already believed in** the validity of **his prophecy. If they had not believed in it they would not have returned in repentance. And his words,** predicting the destruction of **the city would have come to be. And if this is the case, that is what I say to those who say that he was a false prophet. And in addition to this, what does it matter to Jonah if the people of Nineveh say that he was a false prophet or a true prophet? He was not of them or counted among them. After he proclaims his proclamation he returned to his land. So what is it to him or to them that because of this he would flee from before the Eternal and pass up his prophesying?** Also **this** argument **is not according to the edict that at this first time** God spoke to Jonah. At that time **The Blessed One did not say to him the content of the proclamation concerning the overturning of Nineveh. He told him this later** after Jonah returns to dry land. **So** at this point in the story there is no reason **for the prophet to fear that they would return in repentance and say that he is a false prophet. For here He only tells him** *"ki alta ra'atam lifanai, for their evil has arisen before me"* (1:2). **And why should he fear that?** In any case by fleeing **the prophet transgressed His words by destroying His prophecy and incurring the death penalty.**

The third question: In the words of the sailors on the ship who say to him *"Vayapilu goralot v'neidah b'shelmi, Let us cast lots so that we will know on whose account"* (1:7) **this great storm has come upon us. For behold the storm in the sea which the ship encounters is a natural and regular occurrence. And how do the lots provide a true verdict in this matter? And perhaps** the storm **was not the result of the sin of one of them. And the lot had to fall on one of them** who would be innocent in the pureness of his heart and the cleanliness of his mouth. **And thus it says in the Midrash that Achan said to Joshua, "Why do you cast lots between me and my house?" And Joshua responds," I will cast lots between you and Pinchas and it will fall on one of you."** During the conquest of the Canaanite city of Jericho an Israelite takes booty, which should have been destroyed. The Bible describes Joshua sorting out the tribes, then the clans, then individuals to determine who is guilty (Josh 7:16–18). According to the Midrash, this sorting is done by the casting of lots. **And here we could**

consider that perhaps the storm was not because of the human sin. Then what would be the meaning of the lot?

The fourth question: In what the sailors said to Jonah *"Hagida-na lanu ba'asher l'mi-hara'ah hazot lanu ma-m'lacht'cha, Tell us now in regard to whom has this evil befallen us, what is your trade . . ."* (1:8). It is difficult to understand this text from their point of view. For the lot has already fallen on Jonah. And they know that this big storm is because of him. If this is the case why do they return to ask him, *"L'mi-hara'ah hazot lanu, Now in regard to whom has this evil befallen us?"* And why do they ask him, *"Ma-m'lacht'cha umai'ayin tavo mah artzecha v'eizeh am ata, What is your craft, and where do you come from, what is your land, and from what people are you?"* (1:8). And how is it possible to connect the storm to these issues? And concerning the questions *"Umai'ayin tavo ma artzecha, Where do you come from, what is your land?"* What are they here for? For the answer of Jonah is not in response to these questions. He says, *"Ivri anochi v'et YHVH Elohei hashamayim ani yeira'eh, I am a Hebrew, The Eternal, the God of Heaven I fear"* (1:9). This answer is not sufficient for all the questions. And after the questions and their answers the text does say, *"Mah zot asita ki yadu ha'anashim ki-milifnei YHVH hu vorei'ach ki higid lahem, What is this that you have done? For the men knew that he was fleeing from before The Eternal for he told them"* (1:10). If he had already told them, why did they need to ask him again? Additionally, because Jonah did not respond to what they said, *"Mah zot asita, What is this that you have done?"* The sailors had to ask him, *"Mah na'aseh lecha v'yishtok hayam meialeinu, What must we do to quiet the sea from upon us?"* (1:11). And in general all these words, which the sailors spoke, require a response.

The fifth question: In the words of Jonah, *"Sauni vahatiluni el hayam, Pick me up throw me into the sea"* (1:12). For Jonah knew to the core of his being that he had fled from before the presence of the Eternal in order not to go to Nineveh and to not proclaim upon it the proclamation that The Blessed One had commanded him. And now that his sins had caught up with him, could he not be saved from the hands of The Blessed One? Why did he not repent for his sin? Why did he not pray to The Blessed One saying, "I have sinned, I have transgressed. Now I will go directly to Nineveh and act according to your will?" And he knows that nothing, none of his sins, once he has repented would be held against him. And The Blessed One will be merciful and relent from His anger.

And already the captain of the ship has pointed this out. For did he not mean this when he said, "*Mah lecha nirdam kum kara el-Elohecha, What are you doing asleep get up and call to your God*" (1:6). And how did he choose to choke off his life that they should throw him into the sea? Why did he want to remain standing in his rebellion against God rather than turning in repentance before his God. Is this the act of a wise man, a holy prophet of The Eternal? And what will he do to remove his increased iniquity?

The sixth question: In what is said by The Blessed One "*ladag vayakei et-Yonah el-hayabasha, to the fish to spew Jonah onto dry land*" (2:11). In so much as Jonah had strengthened his rebellion not to submit to the presence of The Eternal to return in repentance in the matter of going to Nineveh. Why does The Eternal turn from His anger and command the fish to spew him on to dry land? And if it is because of the prayer, which Jonah prayed from the belly of the fish, how did his prayer help with the seriousness of his sin? He was like a drowned rat in His hand. Since he had withheld prophecy he was subject to death and would not be saved from dying there. And also the words of his prayer contain difficulties. For behold he says, "*Asher Nadarti Ashaleima, What I have vowed I will fulfill*" (2:10). But we have not found anywhere in the book of Jonah that he made a vow which needs to be fulfilled. I will explain the verses in a manner to answer all these questions.

The general intention of this prophecy is to make known that the wisdom of The Eternal stands forever and the word of God is established forever. And so the prophets believed in their prophecy and their mission concerning the future, seemed to them to be true. For no person who is not a liar has learned practical guidance from Jonah ben Amittai who was commanded by The Blessed One to prophesy not to His people but to Nineveh, the capital of the nation of Assyria. Jonah did not want to go to Nineveh for he knew of the future difficulties which would befall the ten tribes of the Northern Kingdom of Israel. Therefore, he closed his soul to God's call for the purpose that the nation of Assyria and Nineveh its capital would be destroyed. Because they would not repent from their sins since Jonah was not there to call to them. And therefore, Jonah fled from going there. And The Eternal, who measured his actions, cast a stormy wind on the sea until the sailors had to throw Jonah, the sinning soul, into the sea. And he was not comforted by being in the belly of the fish as an accused criminal until he is moved to pray to The Eternal to

save him from there, saying that **he would go and fulfill his mission. For it is no wonder to The Blessed One. For all is "like material in the hand of the creator"** (Jer 18:6). And **"everything He wills comes to be"** (Prov 21:1).

Answer to the First Question

1.1 *"Vay'hi d'var YHVH el Yona, And the word of The Eternal"* until *"Vayiru hamalachim . . . And the sailors feared"* (1:5). Abarbanel begins by examining Jonah's lineage. **Our sages taught, in Perek Hechalil** (Bereishit Rabbah 98:11), **that Jonah the son of Amittai was** on his mother's side **from the tribe of Asher. And he was the son of the widowed woman who engaged Elijah to save her son** and he had died. **And Elijah brought him back to life** (1 Kgs 17:19–22). The Bible does not provide the son or the widow's name. Pirke D'Rabbi Eliezer, chapter 33, identifies the boy as Jonah. **But Rabbi Yochanon** (Yerushalmi Sukkah 5:1) **says that he was from the tribe of Zebulun. For he was the one who prophesied upon Jeroboam ben Yoash. As it is written in the** Second **Book of Kings** (14:25) **"Jonah the son of Amittai from Gat Chefer." And that place was in the portion of** the Land of Israel allotted to the tribe of **Zebulun** by Joshua. **As it is written, "from there Gat Chefer"** (Josh 19:13). **Rabbi Levi says it is good that we learned from Rabbi Yochanon that his mother was from Asher and his father was from Zebulun. As it is written, "Zebulun shall dwell by the seashore,** he shall be a haven for ships, **and his flank shall rest on Sidon"** (Gen 49:13). *"Yarech and he fled"* (1:3) **toward Sidon and he was there** by the sea. *"Vayeired Yafo vayimtza oniya ba'ah Tarshish, And he went down to Yaffo and found a ship going to Tarshish."* **And he would be at shore of the ships as will occur in the future when the prophet Elisha will place upon him** the task **to prophesy and will send him to anoint Yehu ben Namshi** (2 Kgs 9:1). According to the Bible, Elisha appoints an unnamed person to this task. Later rabbis identify this person as Jonah.

And because people always believe in the truth of his words he is called Ben Amittai, the son of truth. **And it comes to us from this that he was from the Kingdom of Ephraim,** the northern kingdom, **from before Senacharib destroyed Samaria,** the northern capital, **and after the men of Assyria destroyed the tribes of Reuben and Gad and half the tribe of Manasseh who were on the other side,** east, **of the Jordan. And also after they exiled Zebulun and Naftali. And there can be no doubt that**

the remaining tribes feared and were frightened that the King of Assyria would advance on Samaria and destroy it, doing to them as he had already done to their brothers who he had exiled. And this fear was in the hearts of the wise men of Israel, including Jonah. They did not require prophecy to understand the threat posed by the Assyrians. Therefore let us continue with the matter of Jonah. What is clarified in this story is that which Hashem, The One of Blessing commanded to Jonah.

2. That he should go "*el-Nineveh hair hagedolah, to Nineveh, that great city*" where rested the thrones of the kings of Assyria. It was the capital of their kingdom. And Rabbi Abraham Ibn Ezra, my teacher, explains the phrase "a great city to God" (3:3) to mean that the people of Nineveh had always been fearer of God from the early days. Only now in the days of Jonah had they begun to do that which was evil in the eyes of Hashem, The Blessed One. If before this they had not once been righteous then Hashem, The Blessed One, would not have sent His prophet to straighten them. But this is not correct and is not the truth in my eyes. The explanation of the phrase "a great city to God" is different than the one offered by Ibn Ezra.

It is not appropriate to explain "*U'kra aleha ki alta ra'atam l'fanai, Proclaim upon it for its evil has arisen in my eyes*" as the substance of the proclamation. Rather say that he will proclaim upon it what Hashem directs him to say concerning its overturning if they do not turn in repentance. For all of this is included in the pronouncement, "*U'kra aleha, Proclaim upon it.*" It is in the nature of "proclaim aloud" not to obscure that he will convince them and frighten them.

And this was according to that phrase "*alta ra'atam, its evil has arisen*" before Him of Blessing. This is not to make Him a monitor over them like the heavenly monitoring of Israel to straighten them out and save them from a plague. Rather since it had been directed that because of their sins, the Kingdom of Israel, Samaria and her daughters would be destroyed by the hands of Assyria. Therefore, The Blessed One tries to save Assyria from the evil that has been designated to come upon them as a result of their violence so that He will save Assyria from annihilation. And Assyria will become the instrument of the anger of The Holy One of Blessing to destroy the Northern Kingdom of Israel as it is written, "Ah Assyria the rod of My anger against a godless nation I will send them and against the people of my wrath I command him to take spoil and seize plunder and to trample them down like the mire of the street" (Isa

10:5). **And because of this The Holy One of Blessing wants to straighten out Nineveh the capital** city **of the Kingdom of Assyria. And this is the reason that he sent Jonah to proclaim upon it.** *"Ki alta ra'atam l'fanai, For its evil has arisen in my eyes."* **And not from Hashem's love of them or desire for them. Rather to save them from the evil so that they will be properly destined for pilgrimage festivals of Israel.** Abarbanel uses sarcasm to describe the future role of Assyria in the history of the Northern Kingdom of Israel. **Thus is the first question answered.**

Answer to the Second Question

3. **And here Jonah understands the truth of this matter and therefore concludes in his heart that he will not go to Nineveh so that the people of Assyria will not be saved from destruction by him. For what would be a reason for his going** to Nineveh **to save children of Assyria and cut off the children of Israel? How would he be able to fear the evil that would befall his nation at the hands of the Assyrians and because of that flee from before the Eternal? That would be to say that he wished to distance himself from the Land of Israel the base for prophecy in his thought that prophecy does not extend to outside the Land** of Israel. **And when he would be in an impure land outside the Holy Land prophecy would not begin within him. And he would not be commanded to go to Nineveh. And** he would **not** have **to proclaim upon it the proclamation so that he would not be central to and an instrument in the saving of his enemy. And if Hashem of Blessing would want to save them He could do it Himself as He wished but not by the means of Jonah and by his hand.**

And I will think that this is the direction of the sages, of blessed memory, as it says in the Mechilta Bo **on the verse and they themselves added words found in the Book of Jeremiah. They stated three** positions. **The one sought the honor the father and the honor of the son, one sought the honor of the father and not the honor of the son and one sought the honor of the son and not the honor of the father.** The father being God and the son being Israel.

Jeremiah sought the honor the father and the honor of the son as is written, "We have transgressed, and rebelled and you have not forgiven" (Lam 3:42). Tradition views Jeremiah as the author of the book of Lamentations. **To explain it is that it doubles his prophecy.** He seeks the honor of God and Israel.

And they add to it the words of Elijah that he sought the honor of the father and not the honor of the son. As it is written, "I have been very zealous for the Lord God of hosts; for the people of Israel have forsaken your covenant, thrown down your altars, and killed your prophets with the sword; and I am the only one left; and they seek my life, to take it away (1 Kgs 19:14). And what does it say there? "And the Lord said to him, 'Go, return on your way to the wilderness of Damascus. . . . And Jehu the son of Nimshi shall you anoint to be king over Israel; and Elisha the son of Shaphat of Abelmeholah shall you anoint to be prophet in your place" (1 Kgs 19:15–16). And what does the text mean "in your place?" That it is impossible through your prophecy. Elijah fled to the wilderness from his life of speaking to the people of Israel, "the son" who remained committed to their lives of sin despite his efforts.

Jonah sought the honor of the son and did not seek the honor of the father. And what is written here, *Vayahi d'var YHVH el Yonah shainit, And the word of the Eternal came to Jonah the second time*" (3:1). It says second, a second time He spoke to him. A third time He did not speak to him. According to what I have clarified Jonah sought the honor of the son and not the honor of the father in his flight from before Hashem so that he would not go to straighten out Nineveh. For he chose that the counsel of the Eternal would not come to be. And the Assyrians would be completely cut off. As it is written in the Midrash, Rabbi Yochanon said, Jonah did not go except to lose his life at sea. As it is written, "*Sauni Vahatiluni El Hayam, Pick me up throw me into the sea*" (1:12). Jonah fled expecting that this would cost him his life.

And similarly you find in patriarchs and the prophets people who gave their lives for Israel, like is said concerning Moses "Yet now, if you will forgive their sin; and if not, blot me, I beg you" (Exod 32:33). And what about David? "And David said to The Eternal . . . 'Behold, I have sinned, and I have done wickedly; . . . let your hand, I beg you, be against me, and against my father's house'" (2 Sam 24:17).

And all these verses testify and express the truth of what I have clarified concerning this. And what is written in the Mechilta agrees. There it says Jonah goes to outside the Land of Israel because the Shechinah does not reveal prophesy there. And according to the fact that he knows the nations were close to repentance. And this certainly does not obligate Israel to guilt. There is a story a servant of who ran away from his master, a Priest, saying, I will flee to a cemetery, where the master is unable to go after me. His master said to him, "I have servants like you whom I can send after you to retrieve you from there." Jonah said, I will go to outside the Land of Israel to where the Shechinah does not extend. And The Holy One of Blessing said to him I have servants like you to send after you to bring you back from there. As it says, "*V'YHVH heitil ruach gedolah el-hayam, The Eternal cast a mighty wind upon the sea*" (1:4). The printed Abarbanel text has "*sa'arah*, storm" in place of "*gedolah*, mighty."

And it is certainly good how Rabbi Abraham Ibn Ezra precisely analyzes this phrase. For it does not say he flees *mipnei*, from, from The Eternal, rather it says "*meilifnei*," he fled from before The Eternal. For *mipnei*, from, The Eternal refers to His knowledge and His oversight. How could Jonah flee from this? For it is written, "The fullness of the entire land is His glory" (Isa 6:4). And as it is said "*mipanechah evrach*, from you I will flee" (Ps 139:7). Certainly, the phrase, "*meilifnei YHVH*" describes drawing close to the Eternal and receiving prophecy. As is said, "*Chai YHVH asher amaditi lifanav*, As the Eternal lives, before whom I stand" (2 Kgs 5:16). And as it says concerning Cain, "And Cain went out *milifnei*, from before the Eternal" (Gen 4:16). The Eternal who removed from him his oversight and closeness. As it is written, "From Your face I will be hidden" (Gen 4:14). And in the case of Jonah, he flees in order to destroy his designation for prophecy in order to remove the light of his prophecy as I have mentioned. And this is in order that the children of Assyria, who are in Nineveh, will not be saved knowingly by his hand. And from this, is derived the importance for The Eternal of the evil of the tribes explained above. Thus is the second question answered.

Answer to the Third Question

And with what I have written on this subject to clarify the reason why this story is written about events which took place in Nineveh and included in the Holy Writings in that there is no positive mention of Israel. For it seems to be entirely for the nations of the world. You might think that it is pointless if it is not read to other nations for it describes their possible destruction and death. And if the nations are greatly diverted by this, it is not remembered nor is it written in the Holy Books.

And it is also said that this was written to be moral teaching for Israel who will be hastened to repentance like the people of Nineveh.

This is in truth a very weak reason. For if the children of Israel do not accept moral teaching from the commandments of the Torah and the words of the prophets how are they going to accept moral teaching from the actions of the people of Nineveh? Also it is not recalled in the Bible that in Nineveh they removed the high places for the worship of idols and the idols they continued to serve, for they continuously held to them throughout their repentance. And what is this moral teaching that Israel could take from them?

Rather according to what I have explained, this story is written in the sacred writings not to recall the testing of Nineveh but rather to recall the testing of Jonah and to promote his righteousness and the miracle that was performed for him so that we will know that which God does will be established for all time And Nineveh will recount the narratives that were about heard of the kingdom of Assyria.

And Jonah wanted *"livroach Taeshisha, to flee toward Tarshish"* that is the city which today is called among the Ishmaelites, Tunis.

And it is written *"Vayeired Yafo, He went down to Yafo,"* the land of Israel is higher than all the other lands. And Yafo is on the seashore, closest to the Land of Israel.

And the text says, *"Vayitein s'charo, And he paid its fare"* It was the way of seafarers not to pay the fare for the journey until they exit the ship to the port. Here Jonah close to fulfilling his desire to escape abandons the rest of his work in his boarding it, the ship. Thus in the explanation in Pirke D'Rebbi Eliezer, following the Agadah that Jonah was wealthy and paid the fare of the entire ship, he chartered it, so that it would transport him alone.

4. And since that his going was not according to the exalted will of God, *"Heitil ruach gedola el hayam vayehi sa'ar gedol bayam, And the Eternal cast a mighty wind on the sea and there was a mighty storm on the sea."* And in this the text explains the reason of the storm of the sea. What is it? It is like the philosopher explained that when a mighty wind enters the sea to be the wind that moves from its place, it powerfully attempts to break forth from under the sea according to the nature of its lightness. And the water in its heaviness is strengthened on the wind and in this way it becomes a storm. And it will be after it says, *"Heitil ruach gedola el hayam, And the Eternal cast a mighty wind on the sea."* The text explains the reason and it says *"Vayehi sa'ar gedol bayam, And there was a mighty storm on the sea."* And this is the swirling of the waves. And if

you would say that in nature wind does not enter the sea on its own, that it was not the time that it was ready for this, but the Blessed God in His overseeing cast it there. And thus it produced the storm.

And indeed it says *"v'haoniya chishva l'hishveir, and the ship thought it would break apart."* Since obviously a ship cannot think, **it is possible to explain that the men of the ship thought that the ship would break apart because of the magnitude of the storm. It appears to them that it is breaking apart. But because a ship does not break apart in a storm while at sea, but sinks in it as the sea piles on it. And in truth a ship does not break apart until it reaches land or the rocks which are around the land. Because of this, to explain** *"v'haoniya chishva l'hishveir, and the ship thought it would break apart"* **I say that they feared that it would sink in the roaring waves of the sea and the people on it would not escape. And so** when the text says **the ship was** thinking, **it means to say, its people were thinking. And they tried to row the ship to the land so that it would break apart there in a way that the people could escape. That it is written that they were close to land. Therefore the sailors chose and all of their thoughts were the ship would break apart and that when it would break apart they would be close to land so that they could escape. But because the Blessed God** *"Heitil ruach gedola el hayam, And the Eternal cast a mighty wind on the sea"* **from the dry land, the sailors were not able to return the ship to dry land to break apart there. For the wind was coming from there, and pushed it toward the sea.**

5. *"Vayiru hamalchim vayizaku ish el-elohav, And the sailors feared and cried out each to his own god."* Until the verse **"The Eternal designated the big fish"** at the beginning of chapter two **the text describes that the sailors in their fear of the storm cried out and called** each **to his god. That this is the first way** to save themselves **that people tried at the time of a storm. And when they saw that this was not working they tried a second way in increasing** seriousness. **They threw the cargo that was in the ship into the sea. And you could say** this refers to **the boxes and wares and all the heavy objects in order to lighten the ship and raise it in the water of the sea and not be swept into it.**

And in truth when the text says *"V'yonah yarad el yirkatei has'pheena, And Jonah descended into the holds of the ship."* The problem here is that *"yirkatei*, holds" is plural. The text **means to say into one of the holds of the ship.**

"Vayishkav vayeiradam, He laid down and fell asleep." The text says this to explain that as the sailors cried to their gods Jonah did not cry out to Hashem for he was embarrassed and ashamed to raise his face to Him. So *"Vayishkav vayeiradam, He layed down and fell asleep"* thinking that he would die there. For sleep is one sixtieth of death, and so he prepared himself for it (death).

6. And because of this the *"rav hachoveil"* calls to him and says to him *"Ma lecha nirdam kum kara el-elohecha, What are you doing asleep get up and call to your God."* *"Rav hachoveil* is the master of the ship. And it is as if he says to Jonah, "Don't you see the difficulty of this moment and the great danger in which we stand? How can you not feel it? And if you say that you do not know what to do, act like the sailors. *"Kum k'ra el-elohecha, Get up and call to your God."* You know how to do that. And since they did not know that the God of Jonah would be greater than all their gods. And so they said, *"Ulai yitasheit Ha'elohim lanu v'lo noveid, Perhaps God will pay mind to us and not destroy us."* They mean to say if our gods do not have the strength to save us perhaps if they draw themselves close to the God of Jonah and they are united He will be able to save them. And for this reason it does not say, *"yitasheit ha'elohecha,* Your god will pay mind, rather it says *"yitasheit Ha'elohim, The God will pay mind."* Rather than using the possessive suffix following the general term for gods, text uses *Ha'elohim,* which the Bible never uses to refer to a god but only to refer to *the* God. And he means to say to his (i.e., Jonah's) God and their (i.e., the sailors') gods.

And the word *"yitasheit"* in the text is quite unusual. Targum Yonaton understands the meaning of this word to be from the language referring to mercy. And Rabbi David Kimchi explains it to mean perhaps God will be "willing" to save us. This hitpa'ail verb occurs only this one time in the entire Bible. To understand it Abarbanel turns to a related noun which shares the same three letter root (Eeiyin, Shin, and Tav) found in another biblical verse. *"Ivdu ashtinotav, His plans perish"* (Ps 146:4). It means to say, May God be willing to save us and not destroy us. For concerning the collective groups of gods to whom the people on the ship prayed, the text speaks in singular terms *"yitasheit haelohim,* Using a singular verb form. The text should be understood to mean that one of the gods will pay mind.

7. And when the sailors saw that their prayer and their outcry were not effective and also that the lightness of the ship which resulted from them

throwing the cargo into the sea did not improve their situation. They thought that this storm was a matter set by God because of the suffering of one of them. And it is not proper that a person should think that the sailors threw Jonah into the sea in haste and in a hurry. For they relied on experiences to prove that this storm was not natural but rather it is in the way of God's oversight of the world.

And the first knowledge from their experience as sailors is what is said in Pirkei D'Rebbi Eliezer. They saw other ships coming and going in peace and quiet. And only their ship was in the mighty storm. Therefore their thoughts agreed that the storm was because of the suffering of one of them. Or perhaps the Eternal decreed, or according to the heavenly array, the stars, a certain person was destined to die at that time in the swirling waves of the storm. And if this was the case, it is proper that the person would die at the appointed time. And thus the rest of the people on the ship would not die with him.

And it is not necessary to think as was said that they saw other ships coming and going. That would be in the manner of Drash. For here the verses provide the evidence. This is what it says "*Vayehi sa'ar gedol bayam v'haoniya chishva l'hishveir, And there was a mighty storm on the sea, and the ship thought it would break apart*" (1:4). This verse means to say the ship on which it is known that Jonah is on, that is, the ship that thought it would break apart and not the other ships. And if in the words of the sailors when they said, "*b'shelmi hara'ah hazot lanu, because of who this evil in upon us.*" They mean to say, "to us" not to the other ships. And Jonah also says, "*ki yodai'ah ani ki v'shelmi hasa'ar hagadol hazeh aleichem, it is because of me that this great storm is upon you*" (1:12). And it means to say on your ship not on other ships.

And the second experience is that they did not cast lots only once because if they had cast lots only one time the fact that it fell on Jonah might have been the result of random chance. Rather they cast lots many times and they changed the lots but each time the lot fell on Jonah. And when they saw that despite the changes all the attempts the result was the same they believed that is was correct to conclude that the result was from God and not a random event.

And in this matter we can also rely on what the text says, "*L'chu v'napila goralot, Come let us cast lots.*" And it says, "*vayapilu goralot, they cast lots.*" For behold the lot will tell us which one of us is responsible for this storm. And is similar to "With lots he divided the Land"

(Josh 18:10). After the conquest Joshua casts lots to determine which tribe receives which portion of the land of Israel. When it **says by "lot"** in the singular **it is in truth "lots"** in the plural. **We can say with the many changes in the lots on which they depended, they knew that certainly the lot identified one of them justly. And it is clear that the sailors did not do anything in haste. Thus is the third question answered.**

Answer to the Fourth Question

8. **The sailors do not immediately seize Jonah. And they do not** immediately **throw him into the sea because the lot fell on him. Rather they do an additional third investigation. For they thought perhaps the lot fell on Jonah randomly each time. Therefore they asked him after the lots,** *"Hagida-na lanu ba'asher l'mi hara'ah hazot, Please tell us because of who has this evil fallen on us?"* **And the explanation of this verse according to me is that this is the first of two times** they ask him questions. **The first is that they ask him, "Has he committed a sin for which the punishment is death?"** They want to know **if it,** the life threatening intense storm, **is because of the severity of the sin or because of who he has sinned against. And this is why** the text **says,** *"Hagida-na lanu ba'asher l'mi hara'ah hazot lanu, Please tell us because of <u>who</u> has this evil fallen on us?"* **It means to say, tell us ba'asher,** which implies two questions: **it means to say,** tells us **what was the sin and it also means to say, who among those here** committed **this sin** bringing **this evil upon us. And because of this, these two words "ba'asher l'mi, because of who,"** the text **intends to express through them two questions. And it is not the equivalent of the word *"b'shelmi"*** (1:7) **as Radak thought.** Rabbi David Kimchi sees *baasher l'mi* here as having the same meaning *b'shelmi* in verse 7.

    I have already seen in the commentary of Rashi that he explains this verse **and writes, "Against whom have you sinned that this evil should befall us?"**

    And he, Rashi, **explains another matter their question and their saying,** *"Mah-m'lacht'cha, What is your craft . . ."* **It means to say, "Does that craft,** or ongoing regular activity **contain serious criminal behavior. It is as if an Israelite priest would say to worshipers of idols that they are sentenced to death before God.**

"*Umai'ayin tavo, And from where do you come.*" It means to say, "Do you come from evil parents that the Holy One of Blessing visits their sins on you?"

And these two questions **can be combined in the** one **question** which begins "*Baasher*" saying, "In what sin did you or your parents . . ." Two other questions are recalled in what is written, "*l'mi hara'ah hazot lanu, because of who has this evil fallen on us?*" And they are "*Mah artzecha, v'eizeh am ata, What is your land, and from what people are you?*" It means to say, "Is you sin against the land, for example, disregarding sabbatical and jubilee years?" or "Is your sin against your nation?"

9. Because these questions are combined in the knowledge of the severity of the sin and against who the sin is, therefore Jonah responds to both of them with the phrase "*Ivri anochi v'et YHVH Elohei hashamayim anochi yarei, I am a Hebrew, it is the Eternal, the God of heaven I fear.*" Our text of Jonah uses *ani* in place of the second *anochi*. Both words mean "I." *Anochi* is a more formal form. **It means to say, what you asked, are my misdeed and my sin against the land or against my people? That as a result of it I am sentenced to death. And against who have I sinned is known and seen because** I said, "*Ivri anochi, I am a Hebrew.*" **There the intention** of the text **is not simply to indicate that he was from the land of the Hebrews but rather** it is a play on the word Ivri to mean that he **sinned.** Out of the root (Eiyin, Vet, Raish) one can form the word *Ivri*, a Hebrew, and the word *aveira*, sin. **And he sinned** against **the commandment of his God.**

And from this use of **this expression** we could ask **why did you sin** by not following **the** words from **the mouth of the Eternal. And in this is clarified to them** severity of his sin and against who he had sinned **as they asked him. And against who was the sin? As he responded to them,** "*V'et YHVH Elohei hashamayim anochi yarei, It is the Eternal, the God of heaven I fear.*" **In order to say, "You do not have to ask me about my land, or my nation, for I did not sin against them. But I fear the Eternal. Against Him alone is my sin." And in this** way I **capture** the meaning of the phrase "*Ivri anochi, I am a Hebrew.*" Jonah says, "**For I sinned** by not following **his commandment and his prophecy. For it is the God of heaven, who I fear. And my sin is against Him. And the matter does not depend on the order of the heavens. For if God, who** rules **over them, who has made the sea move and rage against us, and the dry land to which we are unable to draw closer.**"

And the other possible approach to understanding this text is from the explanation that the sailors asked, *"ba'asher l'mi hara'ah hazot lanu, because who has this evil fallen on us?"* In order to say, "Is this evil because of the arrangement and the decree of the heavens because of his birthplace he was obligated to be drowned in the sea? Is it in his stars, or because of the Divine providence? In order to clarify this further they additionally asked what is your craft? And where do you come from? And these are not four questions as they might appear from the plain reading of the text. Rather they want to know in their saying, *"mah malatecha,"* is what actions, what deeds have you performed that in their doing would cause you to be sentenced to this punishment? And they would not ask about his *melacha* if it were a deceitful act or a simple sin. Because *"mah malatecha"* is a question which only makes sense here if it is a deed, an act that in performing it would cause one to be sentenced to death.

And had they said, "If you say that you have not committed any sin, it will be, if that is the case, that your drowning will be the result of the sin of others, your land and its fate. If in the iniquity of your nation in which you dwell lies the cause of this storm. That is what is conveyed by the questions *"Mah artzecha, v'eizeh am ata, What is your land, and from what people are you?"* If so, then, because of their sin you are sentenced to death. Thus if that is the case, then all the questions were included in the two questions. I want to say that *"mah malatecha"* is a question about the specific act, the result of which is the death sentence. The second is *"umei'ayin tavo, and where do you come from,"* which includes the land and nation from which he came. If their bad fate or evil deeds was the source of this trouble about that Jonah could respond to them, the sailors, accordingly. Abarbanel returns to the Ivri/Ovair word play. Since it is a matter action, the deed that he did in his sinning against God is the subject covered when he says *"Ivri anochi . . . I am a Hebrew or I am a sinner."*

He intends to says that the matter is not dependent on his land or his nation. For he says, *"Ivri anochi, I am a Hebrew."* For the land of the Hebrews was known to them as a good land. And even though the people that dwell there bear some sin, the Hebrews come and go on the sea without experiencing trouble like this severe storm.

But Jonah says, *"V'et YHVH Elohei hashamayim anochi yarei, It is The Eternal, the God of heaven I fear."* This refers to providence. All of this is because of providence and it is not because of the alignment of the heavens. And I fear Him because against Him alone did I sin. And it is He who made the sea and the dry land. Everything is in His hand, like "materials in the hand of the artist" (Jer 18:6). **And in this** way **he explains to them** *"ba'asher l'mi hara'ah hazot lanu, because of who has this evil fallen on us."* The storm is **because of the sin of Jonah, this act and deed that he did. Thus he tells them it is a matter of sin that he fled from before the Eternal.**

10. *"Vayiru ha'anashim yira gedola vayomru alav ma zot asita, The people feared a great fear and they said to him, 'What is this that you have done.'"* **In their realization of the cause of their great difficulty in this voyage they asked Jonah another** question. **"What is this that have you done?" It is not** their **only question. Rather it is an expression as if to say, "How could you do such a thing to rebel against word of the Eternal, to flee from before him? And it will be** expressed here as **"What have you done?" As is said by Laban to Jacob, "What is this that you have done that you have stolen away unawares to me?"** (Gen 31:26). Jacob flees from Laban, taking with him Laban's daughter as well as Laban's flock. Laban pursues him. When Laban catches up to Jacob, he challenges him with these same words.

They do not inquire of him to learn the literal answer to the question, "What is this that you have done." *"Ki k'var yadu haanashim ki-milifnei YHVH hu vorei'ach ki higid lahem zeh, For the men* already *knew that he had fled from before the Eternal. For he had told them this."* **And here I have planted within the explanation of this verse** ideas **from the way in which the commentators** portray **Jonah as praiseworthy, that he feared The Eternal. And all that came to him should not be taken to be** a punishment for **a misdeed that he sinned not by his action and not by his deeds. The truth of this was already taught in my earlier explanation as has been said** in the comment to 1:3.

"Vayiru ha'anashim yira gedola vayomru alav mah zot asita? Ki yadu haanashim ki-milifnei YHVH hu vorei'ach ki higid lahem zeh, The people feared a great fear and they said to him, 'What is this that you have done. For the men already *knew that he had fled from before the Eternal. For he had told them."* **And when did he tell** them? The text does not include a description of Jonah explicitly explaining this to the sailors. Rather he said, *Ivri anochi v'et YHVH Elohei hashamayim anochi yarei, I am a Hebrew, it is the Eternal,* the God of heaven I fear." According to all the **commentators, and in every case the first explanation of them and so** *"Vayiru haanashim yira gedola, The people feared a great fear."* **And**

in their saying, "Woe is us for we have rebelled against the word of God by our deeds." And from what he said, "*Ivri anochi v'et YHVH Elohei hashamayim anochi yarei, I am a Hebrew, it is the Eternal, the God of heaven I fear.*" Based on Jonah's words in verse 9, the sailors are able to reach the understanding they express in verse 10 without Jonah explicitly connecting the dots. "*Yadu ha'anashim ki-milifnei YHVH hu vorei'ach, The men knew that he had fled from before the Eternal.*" Abarbanel explains that the phrase "For he had told them" does not refer to some earlier unrecorded explanation but rather to Jonah's words contained in verse 9. **And this** is what **he had told them. And this clarifies these verses. Thus is the fourth question answered.**

Answer to the Fifth Question

11. **And here the sailors with all the lots they cast time after time indicating the guilt of Jonah, like a hundred witnesses, still they did not throw him into the sea.** Rather **they asked him, "*Mah naaseh lach vayishtok hayam meialeinu, What must we do to quiet the sea from upon us?*" It means to say that after you fled from before The Blessed One, how can you repair this? Should we go to the place about which The King,** God, **spoke and cause His thoughts to be brought there?** The sailors suggest that they could fulfill Jonah's mission. **Or you will swear an oath to the Eternal, an oath to the Protector of Jacob to go there and fulfill his commandment? Or is there another way to become obedient to God's will, in order to cleanse you of your sin?**

12. **And he responded to them "*Sauni vahtiluni el hayam, Pick me up throw me into the sea.*" He means to say, "I do not want to go to Nineveh. I do not choose to turn in repentance or to swear an oath to go there, to fulfill The Blessed One's mission. For it seems good to me that you will throw me into the sea and I will die there. From that which appears to you to do to save yourselves, do not cease again. For I know that this great storm is upon you because of me." And here Jonah ceases his repentance and chooses to stifle his soul and die in the depths of the sea so that he will not go to save the Assyrians who will in the future will be aroused** by God **to cause the death of** the Northern Kingdom of **Israel and destroy it. And thus is the case his intention was to serve heaven.** Abarbanel argues that he did not flee out of selfish fear. Rather his flight was motivated by a positive concern for the future of the Northern Kingdom. If he did not go

to Nineveh, the capital of the Assyrian empire, the Ninevites would not repent from their sins. If they do not repent God cannot use them as the rod of Divine anger to destroy the Northern Kingdom. Therefore Jonah flees to save the Northern Kingdom. Even though he faces death he does repent because he remains committed to the larger goal of saving the Northern Kingdom. Abarbanel presents Jonah as a heroic figure prepared to sacrifice himself to save his people. **Thus is the fifth question answered.**

Answer to the Sixth Question

13. **And when the sailors had heard the words of Jonah, his question and his request, they did not obey his instruction,** to throw him into the sea, **rather they rowed and exerted themselves** *"l'hashiv haoniyah el-hayabashah, to return the ship to dry land."* **In order to remove Jonah from it and send him on his mission to quickly deliver the injunction in Nineveh. And The Holy One did not choose this path for Jonah for He wanted Jonah of his own free will to repent and ask to go to on the way, which the Holy One had sent him. And they were not able** to reach the shore **because the sea stormed around them and the wind came from the land. And it held the ship in such a way that it was not able to draw closer to the land.**

14. **And when the sailors saw all of this they did more. And the fourth effort was that they prayed and said,** *"Ana YHVH al-na novda b'nefesh haish hazeh, O please Eternal do not let us perish on account of the soul of this man."* **And their intention is to say, "There is no escaping from this decision whether this man is designated to die for his sin or not. And if he is designated to die** for his sin, **this one man will sin. And towards the entire company of the ship** do not **become angry. Do not let us be destroyed for the soul of this man. For his sinful soul will die in this way** or in a plague or in some other manner. For there is no stopping the hand of The Eternal from striking His enemy and the myriads who curse The Eternal. And why should we be destroyed because of him? And if he is not designated to die *"Al-titein aleinu dam naki, Do not place on us innocent blood."* In that we have sent him into the sea and have killed him and shed his blood for no reason. And do not say that You have no other way to kill him except for destroying the ship he is on. For You are The Eternal, for what You want, You do. And always when You proclaim

it is not an **empty saying. And many openings** exist **to fulfill the Divine will** of destroying Jonah **without destroying us.**

15. **And after all these efforts when the sailors saw that in every way the sea continued to storm about them, they lowered Jonah into the sea. And in truth these words teach that they tried to save him a fifth time. And this** follows **what is said in Pirke D'Rebbe Eliezer** (chapter ten): **"They lowered him into the sea up to his knees and the sea quieted from its raging. They returned him** to the ship **pulling him up to them. Immediately the sea began to storm. They again lowered him in to the sea.** This time **up to his neck and the sea quieted from its raging. They returned him** to the ship **pulling him up to them. Immediately the sea began to storm until they lowered him entirely in to the sea."** They did **these many experiments to know** for certain **that the reason** for the storm **was Jonah. And the sages, may their memory be for a blessing,** came to this understanding **in their precise reading of the words of the text. For it says,** *"Sa'uni vahatiluni, Pick me up and throw me"* (1:11). **This teaches that they performed two discrete actions. They lowered him in to the sea and drew him out of there to see the truth of the matter. And this explains what is said** in this verse *"Vayisu et-Yonah vay'tilunu el hayam, They lifted up Jonah and lowered him in to the sea."* **After they with drew him from the sea several times, finally they lowered him in to the sea to stay.**

16. **And it says that** *"Yir'u ha'anashim yir'ah g'dolah et-YHVH, The men greatly feared the Eternal"* **in their seeing** the **strength of His providence and the greatness of His miracles. And they vowed vows to offer sacrifices according to the custom of those who go down to the sea in ships when they go down into them.** The general practice is for sailors to promise to offer sacrifices upon their safe return. Here these sailors add to those general promises new vows to offer additional sacrifices upon there return. They lack the animals and proper altar to offer sacrifices while at sea.

And in Pirke D'Rebbe Eliezer it says that they converted, and returned to Yaffo and went up to Jerusalem and circumcised the flesh of their foreskins. For it says, *"Yir'u ha'anashim yir'ah g'dolah et-YHVH vayizb'chu zevach, The men greatly feared the Eternal and offered sacrifices."* **The offering which they offered at sea is the covenant of circumcision which is like blood of the sacrifices.** The sailors would first have to become Israelites before they could offer proper Israelite sacrifices.

"Vayirdu nedarim, And they vowed vows" to bring man, his wife, and the children and all that they have to the God of Jonah. And they made vows and fulfilled them. And concerning them it is written, *"m'shamrim havlei shav chesed ya'azovu, Those who guard utter vanities,* now *they will forsake their shame"* (2:9). Abarbanel understands this verse from Jonah's prayer to describe the spiritual progress of the sailors. In this last section Abarbanel draws heavily on Pirke D'Rebbe Eliezer but reworks the sequence and language of that text.

Chapter Two

1 *"Vay'man YHVH dag gadol, And The Eternal designated a big fish."* Until the end of the prophecy the text tells us that in the same place in which the sailors threw Jonah into the sea The Holy One of Praise designated the big fish that swallowed him whole without injuries. And there is no doubt that there is not any way that a person could live in the belly of the fish even one hour certainly not three days and three nights. For a person could not exist in the belly of the fish, unless he is able to breathe cold wind, fresh air, from outside the fish. For there is nothing here to diminish faith in the miracle.

And our eyes see that fetus resides in its mother's belly for nine months without eating, drinking, taking care of his needs, reliving himself, or breathing cold wind, fresh air, from outside. And what would prevent The Eternal from doing so for Jonah for those days? Does not the text of the book of Daniel give testimony that Chanania, Mishael and Azariah, referred to by their Chaldean names Shadrach, Meshach, and Abed-Nego in the third chapter of Daniel, survived "bound into the midst of the burning fiery furnace" (Dan 3:23). And there is no doubt that following nature they would not have lived. For the burning hot air that would have consumed the moisture on which the roots of life depend and the wind would have killed them in an instant but the abilities of God transcend nature.

2. And it was more intense than this—than the experience of Chanania, Mishael, and Azariah—for Jonah when he was in that place (the belly of the fish) his thoughts and his very being were threatened until he prayed from there to God.

3. **And here in his prayer we found** and **we saw that most of his words are in the past tense,** in this verse, *"Karati mitzara li. . . . Shivati shamata koli, I called out in my distress. . . . I cried out, You heard my voice."* And **in all the rest of the verses** of Jonah's prayer. **So people have thought that he did not pray this prayer** until after he **went out** of the fish **to dry land. And Rabbi Abraham Ibn Ezra responds to them that all words of prophecy are expressed in this way.** Abarbanel presents the verses which Ibn Ezra used to prove this point. **And Jacob said, "I** <u>took</u> **from the hand of the Amorites with my sword and my bow"** (Gen 48:22). In the blessing of Joseph's sons, Jacob speaks of what their descendants will one day inherit. This "taking of the land of the Amorites" does not occur until the time of Joshua, nevertheless Jacob uses the past tense to describe it. **"And he bow**<u>ed</u> **his shoulder to bear** and become a slave in forced labor" (Gen 49:15). This is Jacob's blessing of Issachar, again describing in the past tense events that will not occur until after the conquest of the land. Another example, **"A star** <u>came</u> **forth out of Jacob** and a scepter arose out of Israel" (Num 24:17). This is from Baalam's words concerning the Israelites. He is describing the future reign of King David, using past tense verbs. **"But Jeshurun wax**<u>ed</u> **fat and kick**<u>ed</u>**"** (Deut 32:15) and **"And God** <u>saw</u> **it and spurn**<u>ed</u> **them"** (Deut 32:19). These are words from the Song of Moses, through which Moses tells the story of the people of Israel including the future events which will befall the people of Israel. Again in both verses we see past tense verbs. **"So Israel** <u>dwelt</u> **in safety"** (Deut 33:28). This verse is from the final blessing which Moses recites just before his death. He is describing the future of the people, when they will turn away from sin, using past tense verbs.

From this it can be seen that the prayer of Jonah describes what will be in the future. *Ach osif l'habit el heichal kodshecha, But I will look again at your holy palace"* (2:5). *"V'ani b'kol toda ezb'cha-lach asher nadarti ashaleimah, And I with grateful voice will bring sacrifices, as I have vowed so will I fulfill"* (2:10). **So these words come in the past tense in place of the future tense for they were in prophetic visions. And in these visions, these words were proclaimed by The Holy One. They were told as if they had already happened because they were proclaimed in His high wisdom.**

Having presented Ibn Ezra's position, Abarbanel now explains his own position. **For me there is no need for the words of Rabbi Abraham Ibn Ezra,** even though they are **good and straight in his eyes. For in this prayer there is no past tense in the place of the future tense. Rather** Jonah would say **this** prayer **refers to difficulties from my youth. When I** was a little boy death grabbed me. I was ready to be buried. In the days of Elijah *"karati mitzara li el-YHVH vaya'aneini mibeten Sh'ol, I called out in my distress to The Eternal and He answered me from the lower world."* When I was ready to be buried *"shivati shamata koli, I cried out, You heard my voice."* This is a hint to him in this of the miracle performed for him in the days of Elijah that he was brought back to life after he had died. In chapter 17 of 1 Kings Elijah brings back to life an unnamed boy. According to the Midrash Shocher Tov 26:7 and Pirke D'Rabbi Eliezer, chapter 33, this boy is Jonah. And concerning that it is said here, *"Karati . . . Shiviti, I called . . . I cried"* and all the verbs in the past tense. And it is not equal to present tense verbs rather it is a reference to this earlier miracle. Abarbanel sees this entire prayer as referring not to Jonah's present difficult situation in the belly of the fish but rather to his much earlier restoration to life through the prophet Elijah.

4. And it says now He will perform a bigger miracle than that one. *"Vatashlicheini m'tzula bilvav hayamim, You cast me into the depths, into the heart of the seas."* This is a reference to his being in the belly of the fish in the sea. And the river was swirling around him. For joining together there were the waters of the sea and waters of the river. As was written by Rabbi Abraham Ibn Ezra in his comment to 1:4 in a place where the waters of a river join together with waters of the sea there is always rough waters. And to describe his general condition it says, *"Kol mishbarecha v'galecha alai avaru, Your breakers and your waves swept over me."* For he descended under the sea and the waves and the breakers on the surface of the sea passed over him.

5. In addition it says concerning him, *"Va'ani amarti nigrashti mineged einecha, And I said I am driven from before your eyes."* The matter here is that when I, Jonah, descended to Yaffo to flee towards Tarshish, I knew I was removed from before you, I mean to say, that I believed that prophecy would not again be initiated through me. But all my thoughts were vanity. For in truth *"osif l'habit el-heichal kodshecha, I will again see Your holy Temple."* For God will compel prophecy to return to me.

6. It says, *"Afafuni mayim ad-nefesh t'hom, The waters encompassed me to my soul."* And the river *"y'sov'veini suf, whirling reeds."* It is important to tell that the fish which swallowed him descended under the sea in the transfer of him from the mouth of the male fish to the mouth of the female fish (See Rashi on 2:1).

And it says, *"suf chavush l'roshi, the reeds were tangled to my head."* This is similar to the things which grow in the sea which plants acquire. And the reeds grow between them. And sometimes when the fish swim through the water these plants and reeds become tangled around their heads. And it says, *"suf chavush l'roshi, the reeds were tangled to my head."* Now Abarbanel focus on the use of the word "my." **To hint that to the head of the fish that swallowed him that it will descend to the depths,** the text tells us, **the reeds and the plants stuck to head** of the fish. **According-ing to Targum Yonaton, the reeds are a reference to the Sea of Reeds,** which the Israelites crossed leaving Egypt. **And perhaps it mixes with the Sea of Yaffo there.**

7. **And the general matter it addresses with all this is that** *"l'kitzvei harim yarad'ti, to bases of the mountains I descended."* **In that Jonah says,** "I knew that in truth that *"ha'aretz b'richeha l'olam, the land was barred against me forever."* "I mean to say that I would not be able to flee from before You. For the land has bars against me. I mean to say, they are closed and sealed that I will not be able to go out. Therefore this day I remembered that you lifted me up from destruction alive, O Eternal my God. I mean to refer to the miracle that was done for me in my child-hood when Elijah brought me back to life."

8. **And so now** *"b'hitateif alai nafshi, my soul was faint within me."* **Jonah says,** "**In the belly of the fish I remember The Eternal. And I called to Him. And I knew without doubt that** *'vatavo eilecha t'filati el-heichal kodshecha, My prayer would come before you to Your Holy Temple.'''* **That is the heavens.**

9. **So Jonah repents for his sin and says,** *"M'shamrim havlei shav chas-dam yazovu, Those who zealously guard worthless futilities will forsake their kindness."* **He does not say this in reference to the sailors and the people of the ship who vowed vows during the storm. That when they left the ship they righteously fulfilled their vows as the** earlier **commen-tators,** Kimchi, **explained. And it is not as the sages of blessed memory explained** in Pirke D'Rebbe Eliezer **that** *"chasdam"* **refers to the acts of kindness which the sailors did in forsaking their gods because they saw the miracles which were done for them. For all these commentators are distant from the meaning of the text. Rather the truth of the matter is that Jonah regretted that he had fled from before The Eternal. And he concluded in his heart to fulfill the commandment** of God **in the matter**

of Nineveh. But he was comforted by the statement that the people of Nineveh are "*m'shamrim havlei shav, those who zealously guard worthless futilities.*" So even though they will perform repentance in response to his proclamation, they will not remained committed to their repentance for in a short time they will "*chasdam yazovu, forsake their kindness*" and return to their evil ways.

10. And so "*Ani b'kol toda ezvacha-lach, I, with a voice of gratitude will bring offerings to you.*" He means to say, "I will go to Nineveh '*b'kol toda, with a voice of gratitude*' and I will do the proclaiming you commanded." For that will be like a *zevach* and *mincha* offering. For here, this verse, it is heard it will be a good *zevach* offering. And do not think that after I get out of here that I will flee a second time like when I went down to Yaffo to flee towards Tarshish. In truth it will not be like that. For "*asher nidarti ashaleima, what I have vowed I will fulfill.*" And the vow is what he said "*b'kol toda, with a voice of gratitude*" that he will go to fulfill the commandment of the Holy One in Nineveh even though I am frighten and terrified of the destruction of the kingdom of the Northern ten tribes at the hands of the Assyrians. I will not worry about it. I will not be anxious because "*y'shuata laYHVH, salvation is from the Eternal.*" He will save him in His mercy and draw him close in His loving kindness.

11. And remember that it is written that when The Holy One saw Jonah's repentance and that he regretted his sin and departed from the path of sin, and that he swore an oath that would not foolishly flee, then He said to the fish. This means to say that He lifted the wind that was blowing to the shore. He did not literally speak to the fish. He created conditions in nature which caused the fish to move landward.

"*Vayakei Yonah el-hayabasha, And he spewed Jonah onto dry land.*" And in Pirke D'Rebbe Eliezer it is said that fish went 965 parasecs toward the dry land until it spewed Jonah. And because of this nothing stands in the way of repentance. The fish brought him close to Nineveh. And thus is the sixth question answered.

The Second Prophecy

The Second Prophecy begins with "*Vayahi d'var YHVH el Yonah sheinit, And the word of the Eternal to Jonah a second* time." And continues until the end of the book. And it contains two portions of divine prophecy. The first is *"Vayahi d'var YHVH el Yonah sheinit, And the word of the Eternal to Jonah a second* time." **And the second is** *"Vayomeir YHVH heitiv lecha, And The Eternal said is it good to you?"* **And I have asked six questions concerning it.**

The first question: This question **concerns the proclamation which Jonah proclaims in Nineveh in the words of The Eternal,** *"od arbaim yom v'Nineveh nehepachet, in another forty days Nineveh will be overturned."* **And here, this testimony does not come to be. "And the word of our God stands forever"** (Isa 40:8). **And how do these words of prophecy fall to the ground,** how should these words of prophecy understood by the Ninevites**? And if we would say that this testimony of our God is conditional,** depending on **if they would repent or if they would not repent. And this is similar to Jeremiah, "At a moment I will speak** that a nation or a kingdom will be uprooted and pulled down. But if that nation against which I made the decree turns back from its wickedness, I will change My mind concerning the punishment I planned to bring on it. **And at a moment I will speak** that a nation will be built and planted" (Jer 18:7–9).

And there is no doubt that the people of Nineveh were gentiles and did not know the ways of The Eternal. And it was appropriate to assume **that the proclamation would be explained to them,** so that they would understand **that in forty days Nineveh would be overturned if they did not turn to repentance. And this is the way the testimony of our God brings justice and thus the words of prophecy are strengthened. And the nation learns to perform repentance. The testimony is not definite.** It is conditional. **And after** the Ninevites repent, the destruction which Jonah predicted, **does not come to be.**

The second question: Why does the text say, *"Vayeirah el Yonah ra'ah g'dola vayichar lo, And it was evil to Jonah, a great evil and it grieved him."* **For why does it grieve him? And why does his face fall? And why is it thought by him to be a great evil? And what new thought comes to him at this time? For he entered the ship to flee to Tarshish, and he would not do this not except that it was understood and known to him that they would repent and that The Eternal would forgive them** and cancel **the evil He intended to do them. And because of this he went out of the belly of the fish to do it,** fulfill God's mission to the Ninevites. **And at the beginning what was he thinking? And at the end what was he thinking? What was he thinking after The Holy One of Blessing commanded him a second time that he** now **fulfilled his mission? And because of this he went** to Nineveh. **And what is new? If this is now so,** that he accepts his divine mission, **why is he grieved and so greatly angered** by God's compassion towards the repenting Ninevites?

The third question: In his statement, "*kach nah et nafshi mimeni, ki tov moti meichayai, please take my soul from me, for better is my death than my life*"—is there a crazy person in the world who would say what he said? And why does Jonah think **that because Hashem forgave the accused people of Nineveh, He should take his soul and that his death was better than his life? And why should Jonah die as a result of the Ninevites not dying? How does he not cover up his reproachful face from praying this way? Since from the belly of the fish he prayed to The Holy One of Blessing to raise him up from the grave of his life. And he vowed to go to Nineveh to proclaim upon it His decree. And how can he now pray that He will bring death upon him? And this is not what Abraham our father did when he prayed on behalf of the people of Sodom and Gomorrah to save them not to mark them for death. And also pertaining to what Hashem said,** "*Haheiteiv chara lach, Are you greatly grieved?*" **We do not find that Jonah responds with even a word to Him. And this is strange.**

The fourth question: In that Hashem rebukes Jonah, "*Chasta al-hakikayon asher lo-amalta bo . . . , You took pity on the kikayon plant for which you did not labor . . .*" For here this text causes difficulty in two ways. First, because there is a great rebuttal to this Kol V'Chomer argument **that Jonah should** use to **respond to Him, "What is this kikayon plant about which I grieved? It saved me from death. Therefore, I am grieved at its death not for its sake but for my sake. And You say it is like Nineveh but Nineveh did not save You from death, that it does do anything for You. It is not appropriate for you to have pity on it."**

And the second side, in His statement, "*shebin laila chaya u'vein laila avad, which came to life in a night and perished in a night.*" For here His statement, "*Asher lo amalta bo v'lo gidalto, That you did not labor and did not make it grow.*" **The conclusion** is based on the premise **that Nineveh was the work of God from His general creation** of all that exists. **But the kikayon** "*came to life in a night and perished in a night.*" It will be seen that there is no valid **claim in this argument** of comparing Nineveh to the plant, **because Nineveh did not come to life in a night or perish in a night.**

The fifth question: In the statement of The Blessed One to Jonah, "*Va'ani lo achus al-Nineveh hair hagedolah asher yeish bo har-beih mishtaim ribo esra ribo adam asher lo yada bain y'mino lismolo u'v'heima gedola, And should I not take pity on Nineveh, that great city,* *in which there are more than one hundred twenty thousand people who do not know their right from their left and many beasts?"* We will see that Abarbanel understands this phrase, *"more than one hundred and twenty thousand who do not know their right from their left"* to refer to the youth of the city. **And it occurs to The Holy One of Praise to respond to Jonah, "How can I not take pity on these people who come to me with all their heart and all their souls, and in justice, gratitude, having forsaken** their evil, how can I not **grant them mercy? Why does He not remind him of this strong argument rather than reminding him of the weak argument from the youth and the animals** *"who do not know their right from their left?"* **And it is known that because of the repentance The Eternal relents** from his intention to do **evil not because of the** innocence of the **youth and the animals.**

The sixth question: What is the argument from the great number of children and beasts that on their account that Hashem takes pity on the land and the existence of its evil and sinful residents? Does He release the generation of the flood because of the great number of children and the animals which they had? Or does He do so for **Sodom and Gomorrah?** Or does He do so **for the Land of Israel and Jerusalem** in the time of Jeremiah? **Did Hashem,** in the first century, **pass over the evil of its people because of deeds of its sages who did not sin or because of their deaths? If so why does He make this argument in the case of Nineveh? I will explain the verses in a manner to answer all these questions.**

The general intention of this prophecy is to make known that Jonah fulfilled the word of Hashem and his commandment and proclaimed upon Nineveh the decree of Hashem, "*Od arbaim yom v'Nineveh nehpacht, In forty days Nineveh will be overturned.*" And the people of Nineveh were moved from their ways. And they believed in God. And they made repentance with serious intention. And The Eternal had mercy and relented from His judgment. And in response to the grief of Jonah that He did not bring his decree to come to pass, Hashem brought the kikayon to teach him by analogy that if he takes pity on it which he did not create and did not grow, how can Hashem not take pity on Nineveh? As will be explained in the verses.

Answer to the First Question

Chapter Three

1. This second prophecy begins with the words *"Vayahi d'var YHVH el Yonah shainit, And the word of the Eternal came to Jonah a second time"* and continues until the end of the prophecy and the end of the book. Blessed are we that in the chosen words of our sages of blessed memory we find such depth that none of their words fell to the ground unheard. Since Jonah sought the honor of the son, Israel, and not the honor of the father, God, his punishment was that prophecy came to him a second time but not a third time. And it was already thought by one of the interesting commentators, Kimchi, who identified an interpretive approach to his text. We are not obligated to conclude that God did not speak to Jonah again by what it says, *"shainit, second,"* rather than being open to the idea that God spoke to Jonah a third time. But you will find written in Seder Olam that Jonah anointed Yehu ben Namshi to be King over Israel in the year 3062 from the creation of the world. And Jonah lived until Zechariah who ruled Israel in the year 3164 from the creation. From this we can conclude that Jonah lived 102 years after he began to prophesy. And since we do not find any prophesy of his after this long time except for these two prophesies on Nineveh, we know that prophesy from him ceased for this reason. And it is appropriate that this happened. For he fled from prophesy so it was removed from him. His punishment was measure for measure. For prophesy fled from him. And the word of God did not come to him again. His ability to receive prophecy ended and this frightened him. He spoke to him a second speaking. A third speaking He did not. For The Holy One is not stingy in transmitting prophecy but the recipient must be a good receiver. And such is the case with this prophecy.

2, 3. And Hashem commands Jonah after he exits the fish and returns back to dry land to go to Nineveh and proclaim and declare within it the decree which Hashem has decreed upon it. *"Kum leich el Nineveh hair hagedola, Arise and go to Nineveh that great city."* To help him understand His interest in Nineveh, He said to him that because of size of the city The Holy One of Praise paid attention to it. And that is why the text says that Nineveh was *"ir gedola Leilohim, a great city to God."* The intention is not to explain that the people of Nineveh were righteous as was interpreted by our teacher Rabbi Abraham Ibn Ezra. For it was the Land of Assyria. And the nation which dwelled upon it was evil and they sinned against The Eternal greatly. It came to the attention of God because its size. This is similar to other biblical examples of descriptions which connect places or events to God in order to intensify the image. In each case the phrase contains a reference to God that is understood to increase the description rather than to literally invoke the Deity. **In the manner** of **"mountains of God"** (Ps 36:7) is understood as "very high mountains." Or **"an intense flame of God"** (Song 8:6) is understood at a very bright flame **and similar cases.** This interpretation follows Kimchi, who provides these two examples and Psalms 80:11 and Jeremiah 2:31. The text of Jonah uses the term *Leilohim* **for it was** very **large.**

As is written that it was *"mahaleich shloshet yamim, a three day journey."* **And according to plain meaning** of the text **Rabbi Abraham Ibn Ezra wrote that it was a three day walk around the province and a one day walk** across. **And his words are not correct. For the text says,** *"Vayachel Yonah lavo vair mahalach yom echad, Jonah began to enter the city the distance of a one day walk."* **This teaches that he did not cross the entire way for he had stopped** after one day of walking. **Therefore, we can we see that from** city **gate to** city **gate it is three days.**

4. *"Vayachel Yonah lavo va'ir mahalach yom echad, And Jonah began to walk in it one day."* **And immediately its people awoke to repentance. Even though in Bereishit Rabbah it says that Nineveh was a forty day walk. Perhaps it describes the area of the city. And so the decree** *"Od arbayim yom v'Nineveh nehpachet, In another forty days Nineveh will be over turned"* was not pronounced once in one place. Rather Jonah proclaimed the upcoming destruction in every corner of the territory of Nineveh. **For it would be forty days until he pronounced the decree in all the land of the city and its fields. And only then would the overturning** take place.

And this proclamation was pronounced without any conditions. Why doesn't Jonah say, "If you do not repent, Nineveh will over turned in forty days? **What appears to me to say to answer the first question is that the condition in this designation** can be understood **is one of two ways. The first is the straight forward approach, that in forty days Nineveh would be overturned** one way or another. **And this is proven now that if the residents turn in repentance there will be overturning through their deeds of their direction from evil to good, from misdeeds to the most**

righteous of the righteous. And according to the approach which says *v'Nineveh nehpachet, And Nineveh will be overturned"* which follows from the language of a man who is over turned, following *"nehepach libi b'kirbi, my heart has turned over within me"* (Lam 1:20). This verse from Lamentations proves that the Bible uses the term *nehepachet* to refer a profound change in human beings.

And if they did not repent there would be destruction like the destruction of Sodom and Gomorrah. And this approach is sustained from all sides since the word *nehepachet* includes both meanings, overturned and destroyed. And Hashem did not command the prophet to proclaim, "And Nineveh will be destroyed like the destruction of Sodom and Gomorrah." Rather God commanded Jonah to say *"nehpachet"* since God simply wants to show that in time of forty days it will be *"nehpachet."* If it will be in their eyes to perform repentance and "overturn" their deeds in turning to God, then this decree will not be like the decree of God ordering of the heavenly array. For The Holy One of Praise does not rob the heavenly array. God's proclamation to establish it is not conditional.

Thus it says, for the sake of Israel and as a result of its repentance, its prayer, and its crying out, heaven draws close to help it. Certainly for the rest of the nations there will be judgment. God generally oversees them. And when they sin violently and corrupt the paths He determines to overturn them and destroy them like He did to the generation of the flood and the people of Sodom. "For the whole earth was filled with violence because of them" (Gen 6:13). They completely wasted the opportunity of their repentance. And I have already explained this in my book **Mirchevet Hamishnah,** Second Chariot, a commentary on the book of Deuteronomy in **Parashat V'etchanan, the elevation of the nation of Israel over the rest of the nations in the matter of the array** of the heavens. **And that according to the first words that every nation and nation has in general a star and a stellar sign in the heavens. And this is not the case for Israel. For a portion of Hashem, is His people.**

And secondly, also in the fate of the **generations, the individuals of the nation, which are** determined **according to the hour of their birth and their stellar sign. And here the array** of heaven **is not in general Torah on the commandments to be fulfilled and the prohibitions** to be avoided.

And thirdly, and the array of heaven **for the individual person of Israel can be lessened through prayer and merit** of doing *Mitzvot.* Certainly for the rest of the nations the influence of the array of heaven is not lessened by their repentance. Certainly the general divine oversight applies to them to measure their contentious repentance. And thus God sees the existence of the violence between them in general and God cancels this judgment even though they certainly deserved destruction.

Thus is the situation of Nineveh. Certainly the Holy Blessed One protected the nation of Assyria to be his "rod of anger" and "staff of fury" (Isa 10:5) on Israel. God cannot destroy Assyria's capital in the time of Jonah because soon in 701 BCE, God will use the army of Assyria to destroy the Kingdom of Israel. Thus He sent His prophet to cause them to return to the path of goodness. So they will not earn a complete destruction.

And the second way of explaining, "*Od arbayim yom v'Nineveh nehpachet, In another forty days Nineveh will be over turned,*" is that "day" here should be understood as "year." This is like, "It may be redeemed until a year has elapsed from its sale, days shall be its redemption period" (Lev 25:29). Abarbanel provides another case in which the Bible uses the word "days" to refer to years. And the word "*od, another*" and from this counting that comes up to eighty, forty, and "another" forty, and when one adds another forty it will be in total 120 years. And in the end it is as if it said, "In 120 years Nineveh will be overthrown." And that was when Nebuchanezer came and destroyed Nineveh. It was 120 years from this prophecy. And concerning this destruction of Nineveh the prophet Nachum the Elkoshite spoke. The entire three chapters of the brief book of Nahum consist of a prophecy of the destruction of Nineveh.

And the path to truth for us is that Nebuchanezer in the first year of his reign destroyed Nineveh, as it is written in Seder Olam. And it is known that Nebuchanezer became king in the fourth year of the reign of Yehoakim, King of Judah. And it is written in the book of Jeremiah that the fourth year of Yehoikim king of Judah was the first year of the reign of Nebuchanezer. And Yehoakim ruled eleven years. Remove from this four years that were mentioned and we learn that Yehoakim ruled for seven years during the reign of Nebuchanezer. After him Yehochin ruled three months. And after him Tzidkiyahu ruled until the destruction of Jerusalem. Which is fourteen years as is seen in the text. And it is said in the book of Kings that in the nineteenth year of the reign of Nebuchanezer, he destroys Jerusalem and the House of Hashem. And from this we can conclude that nineteen years before the destruction of Jerusalem, Nineveh was destroyed. And it is know that Jonah went to Nineveh after the exile of the land of Zebulan and the land of Naftali and before the destruction of Samaria. And it was between this and that nine years that King Hosea ben Elah ruled until the exile of Samaria. And after this is the matter that Jonah was in Nineveh five or six years before the destruction of Samaria. And from the years of the kings of Judah, we know that the destruction of Samaria was 133 years before the destruction of Jerusalem. We can conclude from this that for nineteen years Nineveh had already been destroyed when Jerusalem was destroyed. If so then from the destruction of Samaria until the destruction of Nineveh was 114 years. And Jonah's journey to Nineveh preceded the destruction of Samaria about six years as I mentioned. And one can conclude from this that from the proclamation of Jonah in Nineveh until the destruction of Nineveh was, without doubt, 120 years. And so it was true when it was said by Jonah, "In forty days Nineveh will be overturned." Hashem, who is Blessed, raised up the truth of the this testimony. And in His intentional use of the word "*od, another*" with the words "*arbayim yom, forty days*" so that the people of the city and also Jonah, would not understand the true intention of the prophecy, the prediction of the future destruction of Nineveh by Nebuchanezer. With this I have taught the answer to the first question.

5. And behold the text reports that the people of Nineveh believed in God. It means to say that they accepted His words and His proclamation. Rabbi Abraham Ibn Ezra wrote in the name of Rabbi Joshua that the men of the ship had gone to Nineveh and spoke there about Jonah and the miracles that had happened at sea. Because of this they, the Ninevites, believed his words without him performing a wonder or a sign. And behold we do not seek a wonder or a sign from a prophet when he commands and clarifies concerning keeping the commandments of the Torah and doing the good and the proper. For also from the mouth of the wise person, who was not prophet, we would be obligated to listen to these words. But if a prophet would command in the Name of Hashem to violate one the commandments commanded in the Torah to be performed at a time fixed. It is understood that it was not an instruction to perform idol worship. In that case, it would be appropriate for the prophet to perform signs to demonstrate the truth of the prophecy. And Jonah explains to them this proclamation concerning their sins in general and in detail about the violence of their hands, their deeds. And

they turned to Hashem. And God **had mercy. Therefore there is no need to ask of him a wonder or a sign.**

But **they accepted the words** of Jonah **to become good and proper from his mouth. Thus it says,** *"v'ya'aminu anshei Nineveh Beilohim, and the people of Nineveh believed in God."* **It does not say that they believed in Jonah.** Or that **the king** of Nineveh **called him** to appear at the palace. **Or spoke to him about this matter. Rather** it says **that they believed in God, that it was in His hand to do all of this,** the destruction of Nineveh. **And that He loves the proper and He hates violence. They are awoken by the words of Jonah to perform their repentance.**

6. **Also the king of Nineveh, who was the King of Assyria, that when he learned of this** prophecy *"Vayakam mikisa'o vayaveir adarto meialav vaychas sak **vayeishev al ha'afar, He arose from his throne and removed his glory from upon him,*** put on sack cloth *and sat on ashes."* The king acts **as if Nineveh was already overturned.** The king's actions are those of a mourner rather than penitent.

7. **And it was commanded to be announced in Nineveh** *"mita'am hamelech u'gedolav, from the counsel of the king and his nobles."* **This means to say, with the people who advise him,** he proclaimed **that the people and the animals will not eat and will not drink.** The people have to repent and fast because they have sinned. Why do the animals have to repent and fast? **And this order applies to the animals even though they do not posses discernment because the eyes of every human being are on them.** The people can learn from the animals. **And Holy One will provide their food in its time. So** now **the cattle in the pens of the city will cry out before Him, so that He will have mercy upon them.**

8. **And the king also commanded that the humans should have no doubt about the** acts of **fasting and the wearing of sackcloth that they do. But rather this sinful people will strongly call out to God. And repent of the violence of their hands. Which is the central issue.**

9. **And in general terms he said,** *"Mi yodei'a yashuv, Who knows perhaps He/he will repent."* Abarbanel presents two ways of understanding this phrase. **This means to say who knows** which specific **act of exploitation and robbery was done by the hand** of which specific Ninevite **that he will repent of it. Or** it could mean **who knows** which of **the paths of repentance** one should follow **to repent before Hashem. So that He will be merciful**

to them. **For in this way Hashem will turn from His anger and they will not be lost. And from this the people of Nineveh feared** God and **understood the Divine decree in terms of its use of the word over turn. For the king had commanded that** the people of **Nineveh would over turn their deeds. So he says to them, perform his spiritual over turning and Hashem will over turn His decree. And the** intended **overturning of the city will not be carried out.**

10. **And the people of Nineveh do not protest. And their king does not worship Hashem, the Honored. And they do not remove idols and im**ages of **gods from their land. For they continually remain strong in their false faith. And it** (the text) **says,** *"Vayar Haelohim et ma'aseihem, And God saw their deeds."* This means to say that in the commandments concerning relations between them and their neighbors, they repented from their evil ways. But they did not repent in their faith. And despite all of this, God relented from all the evil that was to be done** to the Ninevites **for was not the decree** of destruction **concerning the violence of their hands.** One might have expected that the full repentance of the Ninevite described in this chapter would also include them renouncing the worship of idols and the acceptance of the one true God. But the chapter contains no such mention. In an earlier century, Ibn Ezra, also noticed this silence of the text but interpreted it in a much different way concluding that the Ninevites had been worshipers of the one true God all along.

Answer to the Second and Third Questions

Chapter Four

1 **As a result of this** act of Divine forgiveness, *"vayeira el Yonah ra'ah g'dolah vayichar lo, it was evil to Jonah a great evil and it grieved him."* The "evil" **is the sickness that accompanies the grief of his heart. He col**lapses, becomes ill, **feels a great evil, and requests death** from God. **And this is because Jonah thought that** God **would not repent of the decree upon them,** to destroy Nineveh, **unless they repented of their evil ways in faith,** idol worship, **and in deeds,** violence. **But when he saw that they remained strong in their idol worship and that they had not repented in terms of their relationship to God but only in terms of their relationship to each other. And despite this Hashem was merciful concerning**

the evil that existed in His thoughts. And are these categories equal? For idol worship is a more serious sin, than the sins between them. And they did not repent from it, idol worship. So if this is the case, why does Hashem repent from the evil that was spoken to be done to them? There is no other explanation except that He removes their sin and misdeeds and protects them in the pupil of his eye so that they will be the "rod of anger" and "staff of fury" (Isa 10:5) and He will use them to cleanse Israel. And the prophet complains in his heart to Hashem. Why is it His intention to destroy Israel for their practice of idol worship but to people of Nineveh He passes over their similar sin? And this is why it says, *"vayeira el Yonah ra'ah g'dolah vayichar lo, it was evil to Jonah a great evil and it grieved him."* It means to say that he saw in his eyes the great evil that was prepared to come upon Israel. And in the anger of The Holy One of Praise at human beings, He forgives and pities the Ninevites but maintains His wrath on Israel.

2. And thus he prayed *"el YHVH vayomeir ana YHVH halo d'vari ad-heyoti al-admati, Hashem, were these not my words when I was still on my soil?"* And the explanation of his verse in my opinion is not that words which I spoke, I will speak again since I will be alive. It is that all this slowness to anger and goodness that You have done for Nineveh is not out of Your love for them and is not because of justice of their pleas. But rather it is entirely *"al-admati, on my land."* As it says that You are abundant in mercy to the Assyrians so that you will bring them *"al-admati, on my land,"* the land of Israel to destroy it. *"Al kein kidamti livroach Tarshisha, Thus I hasten to flee towards Tarshish."* For I knew that because of my land You would be to Nineveh *"chanun v'rachum erech apayim v'rav chesed, gracious and compassionate slow to anger abounding in mercy."* You will relent on the evil that I declared would occur in forty days. And are not these words, the essence of the prayer of the prophet which are written immediately in the following verse.

3. *"V'ata kach na et nafshi mimeni tov muti meichayai, And now take my soul from me for better is my death than my life."* This means to say that now—after the question of rescue of the Ninevites has been resolved and You will pour out Your wrath on my land and the Assyrians will be your "staff of fury"—since I have already performed my mission, now from my illness which sickens me, *"V'ata kach na et nafshi mimeni tov muti meichayei, And now take my soul from me for better is my death than my*

life" so that I will not see evil you will bring upon my people and the destruction of my homeland.

Now it is clarified that the evil that Jonah feels is not from the forgiving of Nineveh but rather from what he sees as the intention of the Holy One of Praise to do with Nineveh, to use it to destroy Israel. And because of this he requests death so that he will not see the destruction of ten tribes of the northern kingdom by the hands of the Assyrians. And thus I have answered the second and third questions.

Answer to the Forth and Fifth Questions

4. And here Hashem rebukes Jonah for his anger by saying, "*Haheiteiv chara lecha, Are you deeply grieved?*" It means to say that there is an evil aspect to your character that it deeply angers you that I am good to Nineveh. And this is the explanation of Rabbi Abraham Ibn Ezra which he taught in the name of Yaphet ben Ali. And that it angers you that I am good to whom I want to be good. That is not the way of a good person to be angered by the good done by God for, "The Eternal is good to all and His mercy is upon all his works" (Ps 145:9). Jonah should not be surprised that God does good. And the proof of the teacher of this explanation is not found in the response of Jonah to this statement. And if "*Haheiteiv chara lecha, Are you deeply grieved?*" was intended by God to be a question it would appropriate for him to respond to it. Jonah could not ignore a question from God. "*Haheiteiv chara lecha, Are you deeply grieved?*" should be understood as a rebuke from God rather than a question. It is also possible to say that Jonah did not want to respond to this statement even if it was a question. Because he certainly knew that everything is revealed before the throne of glory. And The Holy One of Praise knew the truth of his intention that he was not angry about the good done by God to Nineveh but rather about the future destruction of Israel to come from this Divine act of forgiveness.

5. And still it says, "*Vayeitzei Yonah min ha'ir, And Jonah departed from the city.*" Why does the text here state that Jonah departs from the city? Are we to believe that Jonah remained in Nineveh while the events described at the end of chapter three and in the first four verses of chapter four took place? And Rabbi Abraham Ibn Ezra thought that this had happened after the forty days. And at that time Jonah knew that Hashem had relented from the evil. Ibn Ezra reads this verse as "Jonah had already departed

from the city." **And he thought that from the first reciting of "***Haheiteiv***
chara lecha, Are you deeply grieved?" it is what was said to him after** the
incident **of the kikayon plant. And this is not correct. He says that the
text is not in order as to what is earlier and what is later.** Ibn Ezra argues
that the action described in this verse preceded the conversation described
in verses 1–4. **For there also is the phrase "***vayomeir Hashem haheiteiv
chara lecha, and The Eternal said, 'Are you deeply grieved?'***" repeated.
And** while **it is permitted** to interpret texts in this manner **it should not
be done in this case.**

    **It would be more correct to explain that immediately after the
proclamation of the prophet the people of Nineveh were roused to repent.** They did not wait for the forty days to elapse. **And Hashem informed
Jonah that He had relented from the evil,** while Jonah was still in Nineveh.
"***Vayeitzei Yonah min ma'ir, And Jonah departed from the city***" as to not
fraternize with the evil Assyrians. "***Vayeishev mikedem ma'ir, And he sat
from before the city***," to the east of the city. "***Vayas lo sham sukah, And
he made for himself a hut***" so that he would sit there until he saw what
would become of the city. **For he thought that even though the people
of Nineveh escaped from the general overturning since Hashem had
relented from evil that had been stated to be done. Behold they had not
been cleansed or released from a punishment that could be brought to
all of them or some of them or to the houses of their gods. For in the case
of the golden calf, Moses prayed before he descended from the mountain. And is says there, "And The Eternal relented from the punishment
He had planned to bring upon His people"** (Exod 32:14). **And after this
"And The Eternal sent a plague upon the people"** (Exod 32:35). **And Moses, our teacher, peace be upon him, had to sit on the mountain for forty
days for their forgiveness. And thus was the case of Jonah that he knew
from Hashem that He had relented from the general overturning, he sat
in the Sukkah to see what happen in the city. Would "The Eternal send a
plague upon the people?"** Would God punish some of the people as God
had done in the incident of the golden calf? **Or what** else **might happen.**

6. **And then The Holy One of Blessing prepared the Kikayon plant that
it would sprout there according to the hour. And Jonah rejoiced greatly
for he already had a hut under which he sat. And the sun was shining
through the roof of the hut and striking his head. And as the branches of
the roof of his hut dried he would no longer have shade in it. When the
Kikayon plant came its growth was great and it spread out over the hut**

so that it created much shade, doubling and redoubling Jonah's protection from the sun. **And Jonah was pleased by it. And** the text **says,** *"l'hatzil lo meira'ato, to save him from his evil"* because Jonah was ill with fever as is written above in verse 1, *"Vayeira el Yonah ra'ah g'dolah, It was evil to Jonah, a great evil."* **For he was sick as I have explained. And when the sun would come with all its strength, he might die as he had requested of Hashem, may He be blessed. Therefore, in order to save him from his evil,** his suffering, **this means to say, the evil of his illness and the evil of his request to die, came the kikayon plant. And Jonah rejoiced in it. As is the way of those with fever deriving great joy from cold objects.**

7. **Certainly as it is with the good things of this world, they do last forever. After a short time The Holy One of Blessing prepared** *"tola'at ba'alot hashachar lamacharat vatach et hakikayon, a worm at the dawn of next day and it attacked the Kikayon plant."* **This means to say that it attacked from the bottom so that it would cut off from it the moisture of the earth from below. And this would dry up the upper** parts of the plant **which were source of the shade,** *"v'yaveish, and it withered."*

8. **And it adds to this that in the rising of the sun The Holy One of Blessing prepared** *"ruach kadim charishit, a stifling east wind."* The word *charishit* is not usually used to describe the wind. Abarbanel connects it with the word *charash,* deaf. **As if to say from hearing its roaring until it deafens the ears. And that would be a very hot wind. And behold** *"V'tach hashemesh al-rosh Yonah vayitaleif, And the sun beat on Jonah's head and he fainted."* **As if to say that it brought him to critical condition. Which is the lack of life giving air entering to his heart and the other organs, like the dead.** The heat afflicted him, **until Jonah saw that he had been brought to the gates of death. And he requested** *"et nafsho lamut, that his soul die."* **As if he said to his soul, "Depart from me. For** *'tov muti meichayei, better is my death than my life.'"* Lest I see the evil which has been chosen for my people.

9. **And so Jonah does not request life or health but rather death. And from another side, he is angry over the kikayon plant that "is vanished and gone"** (Song 2:11). **For he had rejoiced in it. As a result Hashem rebukes him with His words** in this verse. **And these two things,** his request for death and his anger at the destruction of the plant, appear to **contradict each other. For He says,** *"Haheiteiv charah l'cha al hakikayon, Are you deeply grieved over the kikayon plant?"* **This means to say, if the situation**

is according to your words that death is good, why are you angry about the withering of the kikayon plant? And it appears that life is good in your eyes. Since you rejoiced in the kikayon plant that lengthened your life and were anger by its removal that brought your death closer. And the prophet responded to Him, *"Heiteiv chara-li ad-mavet, I am greatly grieved to death."* That is to say, I say to You, "Forever I am grieved unto death. And certainly I am grieved over the kikayon plant. Not on the issue of death but rather in terms of punishment and pain I would suffer until I die. And thus death is good but the pain from the sun before death is what angers me."

10. And also Hashem rebukes him on the strength of the matter in His saying, *"Ata hasta al hakikayon, You took pity on the kikayon plant."* You took pity and compassion on this which is not the work of your hand *"shelo amalta bo v'lo gidalto, for which you did not labor and make grow."* And it wasn't anything about which you had previously thought. Since *"shebein lailah haya u'vein lailah avad, it came to be overnight, and perished overnight."*

11. And if so how *"Ani lo achus al-Nineveh shehi ha'ir hag'dolah, Can I not take pity on Nineveh, that great city?"* God says to Jonah, "And it is the work of My hand of which to be proud. And between it's size and strength it is not a Kikayon plant." For behold *"yesh-bah harbei, for it has in it many"* more *"mishteim-esrei ribo adam, than twelve myriads people."* And each *"ribo, myriad"* is 10,000. And it is more appropriate to take pity on them. And you cannot say that you did not pity the kikayon plant in its passing when the worm arrived near you to destroy it for it brought you shade. And what did I receive from Nineveh? Its great name, which is like the shade which the plant brought you. And if you say that they practiced idol worship and did not repent from it, I say they are like human beings who do not speak. For they do not have Torah and are not commanded by it. And there is a portion of Hashem in host of heaven for all nations. And because of this it is not appropriate to punish them.

And because of this He said to Jonah, *"yesh-bah harbei mishteim-esrei ribo adam asher lo yada bein-y'mino lismolo uv'haimah rabah, for it has in it many more than twelve myriads people who do not know their right from their left and many beasts."* And He does not say this in reference to infants as other interpreters, Rashi and Kimchi, have said. For in this condemned city the infants were judged for the sins of their parents for they are like limbs of the adults and their fate is the fate of the adults of the city. But He says this about the population of Nineveh in general. For in the city there are more than 120,000 people without the benefit of the teachings of the Torah. So in the matter of idol worship, they do not know their right from their left. And they are like many beasts. And certainly Israel which stood at Mount Sinai and was commanded concerning idol worship, and heard from The Mighty One, "You shall have no other gods besides me" (Exod 20:3). It is not appropriate to excuse them in the matter of idol worship like the people of Nineveh are excused. It is clarified that this Divine commitment to save Nineveh was strong. And it is supported from the Kal Vachomeir, a "weak and strong" argument, which The Holy One of Praise used on Jonah from the kikayon plant. It is straight and sure and there is no refutation to it. As a general point, also, Jonah enjoyed the kikayon plant like a son enjoys his father who loves him and protects him. Hashem, who is Blessed, loved Nineveh. He caused it to be, and to continue and to thrive. And thus if the God of Blessing is like a father to Nineveh, and Jonah is to the kikayon plant a sort of son, and it is known that the mercy of the father for the son is much greater than the mercy of son for the father. And this is a strong Kal Vachomeir argument. And by what I have explained in this section I have answered the fourth question. I have also answered the fifth question.

Answer to the Sixth Question

And The Holy One of Praise does not respond to Jonah with a mention of the repentance of the people of Nineveh. Since it was not a complete repentance. As they were always practitioners of idol worship they are diminished by their religious beliefs. Thus I have answered the sixth question.

It was not the claim of Hashem, Who is Blessed, to save Nineveh on account of the children and the beasts. For if the nation which dwells, there was a nation similar to a jackass, the metaphor of beasts would be fitting.

And since they are not deserving destruction because of their religious beliefs, since they were not commanded concerning them. Certainly idol worship was not Israel's only sin. For they also committed the following sins: **illicit sex, spilling blood, perverting justice, false measure of volume, false measure of weight, and all the other categories of sin which the prophets recalled. And therefore they are not forgiven. And in light of all of this The Holy One of Blessing does not destroy them,** the Ninevites, **like the overturning of Sodom and Gomorrah. For He lightens their punishment, in His mercy and the abundance of His loving kindness.**

And this is my explanation of this prophecy. With these words, Abarbanel concludes his commentary to the Jonah text. He continues on with a comment on a connected rabbinic text.

In the Talmud in **second section of Maschechet Taanit** 16a **we are taught the order of the fast when they bring out ark to the street of the city. They place ashes of cinders of the top of the ark and on the head of the Nasi and the head of the Av Bet Din,** the leaders of the rabbinic court. **And everyone afterward takes and places** ashes **on his head. And the elder among them declares before them these words, "When our brothers repented,** putting on **sackcloth and fasting did not cause** God to forgive them. **But rather repentance and good deeds caused** God to forgive them. **It is not said concerning Nineveh that God saw their sackcloth and their fasting. Rather it says,** *"V'yar Ha'elohim et-ma'aseihem ki-shavu Midarkam hara'ah, And God saw their deeds that they turned from their evil ways"* (3:10). Another point of view is offered. **And it says,** *"yitkasu sakim ha'adam v'hab'hemah, and they covered themselves with sackcloth, man and beast."* **And in Gemara it says, "What did they,** the Ninevites, **do? They tied the animals separately and the children separately. And they said before Him, "Master of the universe if you do not have mercy on us, we will not have mercy on these** animals and children." This Talmudic sage cannot accept the idea that the Ninevites merited God's forgiveness. So he imagines them evading destruction by taking hostages and threatening God.

And a few other topics are discussed there. And in Pirke D'Rebbi Eliezer concerning the repentance of the people of Nineveh we can learn that for sinners it is the way of Hashem to perform for them a complete repentance.

And behold according to the regulation of the Haftarot they added to this prophecy the last three verses of the prophecy of Micah. The book of Jonah is read as the Haftarah portion on Yom Kippur afternoon. In order to provide a Nechemta, a more positive redemptive conclusion for the Haftarah, these three verses from the end of book of Micah are read immediately after the final verse of the book of Jonah. Abarbanel weaves these verses into the Jonah story.

And they are "Who is a God like you . . ." (Mic 7:18–20). Their subject is that The Holy One of Praise did not pass over the sin of Nineveh, completely forgiving. But rather He postpones expressing His anger until their later destruction of Nineveh by Nebuchadnezzar. But to Israel, in their repentance, it is not thus. For He is forgiving iniquity and remitting transgression absolutely. As it says, "Who is a God like you, forgiving iniquity and remitting transgression passing over the sin to the remnant of His possession" (Mic 7:18).

Because they were His possession and His people, "He has not maintained His wrath forever, because it is loving kindness He desires" (Mic 7:18) to do for them. And He does not act that way with the rest of the nations who sin in their souls. Therefore, it is desired by Him that "He will take us back in love and cover up our iniquities" (Mic 7:19).

And at the time of the future redemption, He "will give truth to Jacob and loving kindness to Abraham" (Mic 7:20). Here He begins with Jacob even though he is the last of the patriarchs. And He does not recall Isaac. Because the point of this verse is that, The Holy One of Blessing "will give truth to Jacob" in giving it to his children. And the loving kindness He gives to Abraham is the inheritance of the land of the seven nations, "the Hittites and the Girgashites and the Amorites and the Canaanites and the Perizzites and the Hivites and the Jebusites" (Deut 7:1). And it is as if He said, I "will give truth to Jacob" from the loving kindness which I did for Abraham. For I did loving kindness for him when he stood before Me between the pieces (Gen 15:1–21). And the truth He establishes with all the sons of Jacob. But not with all the sons of Isaac which would have included Esau. And certainly in order to include Isaac with the rest of the patriarchs, it says, "that You promised to our fathers in days gone by." For with each of the three of the patriarchs, You swore an oath with them.

And thus concludes the explanation of the prophecy of Jonah with the additions of the verses that are attached to them in the order of the Haftarot.

Praise to The God who is Blessed.

5 Malbim

INTRODUCTION TO THE COMMENTARY OF THE MALBIM

MEIR LEIBUSH BEN YECHIEL Michel (1809–79), widely known by the acronym of his name Malbim, lived in Eastern and Central Europe. He was a staunch defender of traditional Judaism in the modern age. He served many communities as rabbi, often clashing with community leaders who wished to modernize Jewish worship and religious life. Born in Volochisk, Russia, and educated in Warsaw, he was rabbi in Wreschen (Prussia), Kempen (Prussia), Kherson (Ukraine), and Moghilev (Belarus). His most prominent position was as Chief Rabbi of Bucharest.

Between 1845 and 1870 the Malbim wrote a commentary on the entire Hebrew Bible. This was the first such effort since the Middle Ages. In his commentary to the book of Jonah we will see his resistance to modernist tendencies. The Malbim takes the Midrash seriously.

All of the commentators deal with the discrepancy between 2:1 and 2:2 in the word used for the fish. In 2:1 the text uses the masculine form *"dag"* and in 2:2 the feminine form *"daga."* Rashi drew on a Midrash from Pirke D'Rabbi Eliezer based on reading the text as referring to two fish, one masculine and one feminine. Abraham Ibn Ezra, David Kimchi, and Isaac Abarbanel all reject this approach as fanciful and unnecessary. The Malbim reaffirms the interpretation found in the Midrash.

The Malbim often refers to the commentary of Isaac Abarbanel, sometimes to disagree with it and other times to affirm Abarbanel's explanations.

Among the interesting new ideas which the Malbim presents is a distinction between Divine rebuke and prophecy. The Malbim argues that Jonah could flee in chapter one because God had not placed the words of prophecy in his mouth. That does not happen until God's second call to Jonah in chapter three.

COMMENTARY TO JONAH OF THE MALBIM

Malbim begins each section of this commentary with a series of questions.

Chapter One

Verse 2

We have not found in any place else in the Bible **that the Eternal sent a prophet of the Children of Israel that he should specifically go to a** non-Israelite **country of the nations** of the world **to bring them back in repentance** to the Eternal. **For it is unique to Israel that the Divine Providence falls upon them, as the sages of blessed memory wrote. And the biblical text explains "For these nations which you are about to dispose, give heed to soothsayers** and to diviners, **but as for you** the Eternal your God has not allowed you to do so. **A prophet** from among you, from you brethren, like me (Moses) will the Eternal your God will raise up, to him you will listen" (Deut 18:14–15). **How is the case of Nineveh different that God sent Jonah?**

Why did Jonah not listen to the voice of the Eternal? And should he not have **run in joy to bring these human beings back from their evil ways? And what was in it,** Jonah's decision to flee, **that they were not of the children of Israel? And how did Jonah defy the word of the Eternal to suppress his prophecy? And** is it not the case that **a prophet who suppresses his prophecy is condemned to death?**

Why does the text **say, "proclaim upon it"** (Jonah 1:2), **but does not explain what he is to proclaim? And the second time** that God speaks to Jonah (in 3:2), God **says, "Proclaim upon it the proclamation that I will tell you."** Again the text does not contain the intended proclamation.

Verse 3

Why does Jonah flee towards Tarshish? If it is so that the word of the Eternal will not reach him, has not the Eternal already commanded him

and he refused to go on his mission? And why should I care if he refused once or if he refused twice?

Why does he flee to the sea and not to the wilderness and from there to outside the Land of Israel? Is not the sea ready for prophecy? As it is written that God's word was revealed to Ezekiel outside of the Land of Israel. Is it because of this that he fled by sea?

And the language of the phrase *ba'ah Tarshish* is not proper for doesn't it want to say that the ship is going to Tarshish?

1. "*Vay'hi d'var YHVH el Yona, And the word of the Eternal came to Jonah.*" Malbim first identifies Jonah by exploring his lineage. Our sages taught in Perek Hechalil (Bereishit Rabbah 98:11) that Jonah the son of Amittai was on his mother's side from the tribe of Asher. And he was the son of the widowed woman who engaged Elijah and asked him to bring her son back to life (1 Kgs 17:19–22). And on his father's side he was from the tribe of Zebulan. As it is written in the Second Book of Kings, "Jonah the son of Amittai from Gat Chefer" (14:25). And Gat Chefer was in the borders of Zebulun according to Joshua 19:13.

Malbim now turns to other mentions of Jonah, first in the Midrash then in the Bible. Malbim understands those episodes in Jonah's life as having taken place before the events described here in the book of Jonah. And it is explained there in Kings that he was the one who anointed Yehu as our sages have taught. According to the Bible, Elisha appoints an unnamed person to this task. Later rabbis, in Seder Olam 19, identify this person as Jonah.

And he was the prophet to Yeroboam ben Yoash who "restored the border of Israel from the entrance of Chamat as far as the Sea of the Arabah" (2 Kgs 14:24). But this does not help because Israel does return in repentance until they prepare to go into exile by the hands of the king of Assyria. By then Assyria was already ruling over them. And this, Jonah's previous positive service, is why the Eternal spoke to him.

2. "*Kum leich el Nineveh u'kra aleha, Arise go to Nineveh and proclaim upon it.*" So that they will return in repentance. The mission was not for the benefit of the people of Nineveh. For we have not found another case in which the Eternal sent a prophet from Israel to cause idolaters to return in repentance. It certainly is not the intention of the Eternal to send prophets only to Israel. Rather God's concern for Nineveh is really out of concern for Israel. After Jonah's prophecy Assyria will be prepared

to be a rod of The Eternal's anger to punish Israel who have obligated themselves to God (i.e., who deserve punishment). The Eternal wants to cause the Assyrians to return in repentance so that they will be ready to fulfill His decree on Israel. And so that the cynic will not ask why did God choose the **faithless** Assyrians **to uproot** the Israelites, it would seem to be **evil** people **destroying those more righteous than themselves. The Eternal wanted to demonstrate that Assyria possesses greater merit than Israel. For they hearken to the words of the prophet and repent. And Israel stiffens their necks** to avoid **hearkening** to the call of the prophets.

When Jonah understood that this mission would lead to evil for Israel, he thought of the importance of not going on this mission. And he rather chose to lose himself at sea rather than being the one to bring evil to Israel. And thus has written Rabbi Yitzhak Abarbanel that for this reason our sages said that Jonah sought the honor of the son and did not seek the honor of the father. He gave his soul on behalf of Israel (as it is written in the Mechilta chapter 21) For in this** sacrifice **depended the rescue of Israel and its honor for the two reasons recalled.**

And so in the first time God called Jonah, as described in chapter one, **there was not sent through him a specific prophecy like the second instance,** as described in chapter three. There **He said to him "Proclaim upon it the proclamation that I will tell you." Which is what he proclaimed, "In forty days Nineveh will be overthrown." After this** proclamation **we do not seal such a judgment** of destruction, for here there remain the possibility of repentence. **And he was not sent in the role of the prophet to announce such a severe decree. If he was sent in this case** to deliver decree of destruction he **would not have defied the words of the Eternal. For the prophet who suppresses his prophecy is condemned to death. So if God only said simply "proclaim upon it" we might think that the proclamation would have been ethical teaching and words of rebuke to turn them from their sins** not a prediction of the destruction of the city.

He explains to him *"ki alta ra'atam l'fanai, proclaim upon it for its evil has arisen in my eyes."* The hour that the evil increases to an overflowing amount, the evil rises up before the Eternal to denounce them. So their evil comes and denounces them. And at the moment that He seals the decree of judgment the evil diminishes for the decree fully resolves the issue from above to below. And so still the decree is not fully resolved only the evil denounces them and he is sent to rebuke them. He does not announce to them the decree. Therefore Jonah thought that this was not a case of a prophet suppressing his prophecy because he was not being sent to prophesy rather to rebuke. **And thus** by fleeing he only **fails to observe the positive commandment which the Eternal commanded him** to go to Nineveh and **rebuke.** With this explanation of the difference between what is technically "prophecy" and what is merely "rebuke" Malbim seeks to diminish the severity of Jonah's sin.

3. **And thus** "*Vayakom Yonah livroach Tarshisha, And Jonah arose to flee towards Tarshish.*" **Out of the fear** that God would **send him a second time and place the word of prophecy in his mouth and send him in the role of a prophet and then he would be obligated to go. Therefore he hastened to flee from before the Eternal.**

And already Rabbi Yitzhak Abarbanel expressed the view that there is difference between *mipnei* YHVH **and** "*Milifnei YHVH.*" Using the phrase *mipnei* YHVH **would speak of** God's **knowledge and sight. How would it be possible to flee from the sight of the Eternal so he does not flee** *mipnav.* **But** *lifnei* YHVH refers not directly to God but rather to **the devotion and inspiration of the Shechinah which exists and proceeds** *lifnei* YHVH, before the Eternal and adheres to the Eternal.

He wants to flee to outside the Land because there the Shechinah does not observe, and from there he will not be sent to prophesy. He chose to descend by means of the sea and not to flee to outside the land through the wilderness because prophecy sometimes occurs outside the land. As the spirit once came upon him in the land of Israel. As is written concerning what happened to Ezekiel who prophesied the word of the Eternal outside the Land because he had previously prophesied in the Land of Israel. And Elijah in his flight to the wilderness from Jezebel saw a vision of God on Mount Horeb. Therefore Jonah climbed on the ship. He thought that at the moment he reached the ship the spirit of the Eternal would not come upon him. And because those who go down to the sea do not focus on the danger of the sea until they arrive at dry land, as the sages have written, and because then he would not be isolated. For on the ship were idolaters and all this would prevent the Shechina from coming upon him.

"*Vayareid ba lavo imahem Tarshisha, And he went down to it to go with them to Tarshish.*" For he wanted to go with them in their company. For our sages have already explained that he paid the price of the entire ship "*vayitein s'chara, and he paid its fare,*" as it is written, "*vayimtza oniya ba'ah Tarhish, and he found a ship going Tarshish.*" It wants to say that the ship was going to Tarshish but the text only says that the ship was just now coming from Tarshish. It is the way of ship masters not to immediately depart on the day of their arrival. Rather they wait for a few days until they find a sufficient number of people wanting to cross the sea in that direction that they combine to pay the full the cost of the ship. And Jonah was in a hurry so he paid the price of the entire ship. And he had in this desire to hurry two intentions, so that the ship would leave immediately and so that there would not be found on the ship many people for he knew that the passengers on the ship would be in danger and he did not want many souls to be lost.

4. "*VYHVH heitil ruach gedola el hayam, And the Eternal cast a mighty wind on the sea and there was a mighty storm on the sea.*" It is clear that this wind was not a natural occurrence, for it was not the season of storms. Only the Eternal controlled it with divine attention. Often a storm comes to the sea from the dry land and so the wind returns on one side and drives the ship to the opposite side and such a wind is found it all portions of the sea. But this wind came from the depths of the sea, from the water itself. At times the winds come from the depths of the water. And it was around this boat. And as our sages have already taught, in Pirke D'Rabbi Eliezer, the other ships passed by in peace for it was not a general wind. Because of this the sailors felt that a punishment had fallen upon them.

And what has been written regarding "*V'haoniyh hashva l'hishaveir, And the ship thought it would break apart*"? Rabbi Yitzhak Abarbanel wrote that the ship would not actually break up, it would sink into the heart of seas. It would only break up if the wind sent it into the rocks on the shore. To this point he explained that the people of the ship feared that the ship would sink in the open sea. And from its impending destruction they thought of the idea to divert the ship to the land so that it would break up there. In this manner some of them would be saved by being close to dry land when the ship would break apart. Does the text not later say, "The men rowed hard to return to dry land?" (1:13). And it is clearly written in the biblical text "The east wind has wrecked you in the heart of the seas" (Ezek 27:26). Because the wind destroys the mast and the sails of the ship. And they are the key elements of the ship. And this is written in BT Gittin 28b.

Questions

Verse 5

After he saw the danger could he not have repented from his sin by say-ing, "I have sinned" and saying to the crew of the ship that they should take him in the direction of Assyria so that he could fulfill the word of the Eternal and not lost his life in the sea for no reason?

Why did he go down into the holds of the ship? Did he not know that at the moment a ship sinks those in the holds are the first to die? From what is said here they, the sailors, are on the ship above, on the deck, where they could be saved after the ship breaks apart by holding onto a plank or something like it. And why does Jonah ask for death?

Verse 7

What is the advice in the throwing of the lots? Did not the lot have to fall on one of them? And how does this make it clear that he had sinned? Is it not possible that the storm came for all of them? In that case the lot still would have fallen only on one of them.

Why does the text say, "*vayapilu goralot*, they cast lots" in the plu-ral? Should it not say, "They cast a lot" in the singular? The text indeed uses the singular, one lot, in the last part of the sentence.

Verses 8 and 9

Why do they ask all these questions? He does not reply to all of them. What he does say, "*V'et YHVH Elohei hashamayim anochi yarei, It is the Eternal, the God of heaven that I fear*," is not an answer to their questions.

And concerning the words *basher l'mi* we do understand their meaning.

5. "*Vayiru hamalachim, And the sailors feared.*" Out of their fear each man cried out to his god in the belief that this anger came from the wrath of their god. They also took personal actions, they threw "*et hakeilim asher b'oniya el-hayam, the ships wares into the sea,*" in order to lighten the ship and raise in the water of the sea so that it would not sink.

Surely "*Yonah yeired el yirketei has'fina, Jonah descended into the holds of the ship.*" And when he feared that the ship in moment would sink, it was his intention that he would fall into the sea. There was a possibility that the Eternal would command the waves of the sea to sweep him from wave to wave until it brought him to dry land as happened to Rabbi Akiva in BT Yevamot 121. Therefore he went down into the holds of the ship.

And there is difference between an *oniya* and *sefina*. A *sefina* is a category of *oniya*. It has a deck and is enclosed above. This is a room underneath in this type of *oniya* from which one would not fall into the sea. Water only comes from the sea into the room **and anyone** in the room drowns there. (This is like the permission to remarry **given in the Questions and Answers of the Mabit**—Moshe ben Yosef Tarani—**to women whose husbands drowned in the room of the Sefina. He did not have a water judgment,** no one saw him drown, **but there is no doubt that the water of the sea entered the room** and he drowned in the closed room.)

And there is another possible **reason for this,** for Jonah descending into the hold of the ship, **for he knew that the storm was on his account and that if he died first the storm would cease saving the men of the ship. So he descend into the hold of the ship where the water would first enter the ship suffocate him, thus saving the men of the ship who be standing above** on the deck.

6. "*Vayikrva alav rav hahoveil, The head of those who seize drew close to him.*" He is the captain of the ship. He has lost all hope of saving the ship through natural means. And he thought that this strange storm which had come only on this ship was the result of a supernatural **decree which had been determined for the men of the ship. And when they all will call out to their gods they each imagine that** their god **would cancel the decree. But when one of them remains silent and does not cry out to his god, the decree remain in force upon them and the ship will sink on his account.**

For this reason the text continues "*Kum kara el elohecha ulai yitasheit, Get up and call to your God.***" The explanation** of *yitasheit* is that **his god would change** his thoughts **to a different thought and cancel the decree of destruction.** The verb *yitasheit* is difficult to understand. Malbim follows the lead of Rashi and others who connect *yitasheit* with "*eshtonotav, his thoughts*" from the Psalms (146:4).

7. "*Vayomeir ish el rei'eihu l'chu v'napila goralot, And each man said to his neighbor* come let us cast lots." **Afterwards they agree to cast lots by this means they would know** "*b'shel mi hara'a hazot, because of who this evil in upon us.*" **The explanation** of why the text uses the plural "lots" **is that they cast lots several** times. **After this if the sin hung on them all then each time the lot would fall on a different person. Then they would know that they are all guilty.**

And behold this could teach that although the lot falls on one man he is not guilty and the storm is not on his account. Only that he knows who is guilty and what he has done to cause this evil. This would include what is written "*v'neida b'shelmi hara'a hazot,* so that they would know because of who is this evil." **For this man upon whom the lot fell, either the evil is because of him or he knows for whom is the evil.**

Malbim now returns to the question of why the plural is used to describe the lots. **And** the text tells **they cast many** "*goralot, lots,*" and each time "*nafal hagoral al Yonah, the lot fell on Jonah,*" **and not on his shipmate.**

8. "*Vayomru eilav hagida na lanu ba'asher l'mi hara'ah hazot lanu, And they said to him, 'Please tell us because of whom is this evil upon us?'*" They ask two questions 1) In the case that he himself is the sinner they say "*Hagida na lanu ba'asher hara'ah hazot lanu, And they said to him, 'Please tell us because* of what *is this evil upon us?'*" leaving out "*l'mi,* for whom." **Asking, "What is the sin that you have sinned on account of which this evil is upon us?"** 2) **And in the case that he is not the sinner but only knows who the sinner is they say,** "*Hagida* na lanu ba'asher *l'mi hara'ah hazot lanu, Please tell us because of whom is this evil upon us?*" including the word "*l'mi,* for whom." The text **wants to say, Who among us is the cause** of this evil?

And it adds "*Mah malecht'cha v'chulei, What is your trade and so forth?*" **Because early people believed that there was a special master who was the god of the sea. And they foolishly believed that he had a hatred for particular type of seafarers and would not allow them to cross the sea. And because of this they ask, "*Mah malecht'cha, What is your trade?*"**

And they say that he has a hatred of particular places and he will not allow people of those places to enter the sea in peace. **And therefore** the text **says, "*mei'ain tavo, from where have you come?*"**

And he has a hatred of particular lands, that he hates the inhabitants and special nations. As is known of the foolishness of the early peoples for this reason they ask, "*Mah artzecha v'eimize am ata, What is your land and from what people are you?*"

9. "*Vayomeir aleihem Ivri anochi, And he said to them, I am a Hebrew.*" This is a general answer to all their questions that he is a Hebrew. Jonah means to say that often Hebrews are travelers on the sea in ships. And the sea does not oppose them, not their land, not places in their land, for they live on the shores of the sea. And concerning the question, "*mah malecht'cha, what is your trade?*" he says to them, "*et Elohei hashamayim ani yarei, The God of the heavens I fear.*" He is a prophet of the supreme God and the sea would not oppose his work and it would be in awe of his God. For The Eternal "*asa et hayam v'et hayavasha, made the sea and the dry land.*" And he rules over rise of the sea. And this was an answer to the other four questions. And certainly answered to the central issue of the questions they asked, "For what reason is this evil upon us?" For he informed them, that he was fleeing from the presence of the Eternal as is written in the next verse.

Rabbi Yitzhak Abarbanel explained concerning what is written "*et YHVH Elohei hashamayim ani yarei, The Eternal, the God of heaven I fear.*" Jonah means to say that I fear the punishment that God will mete out for my flight from before His presence.

10. *Vayiru haanashim yira gedola, The people feared a great fear.* For what is written at the earlier in verse 5 that "the sailors feared" that was a fear of danger of the ship breaking apart in the storm. But this fear is the fear of the Eternal which is great and uplifting according to the greatness of the essence/strength which he permits to flow from him.

"*Vayomru eilav mah zot asher asita, And they said to him, 'What is this that you have done?'*" Look at the commentators who read this as a rebuke of him for the evil of his deeds. I want to say that is a question, "How could you have done such an evil thing to flee from the presence of the Eternal?"

And I explain "*ki yadu zot mipnei sh'higid lahem, they knew because he had told them,*" as is said above in the previous verse.

Questions

Verse 11

And what is the meaning of **the question** *"Mah na'ase l'cha, What should we do with you?"* **Have they not already cast lots to know whom to throw into the sea according to their custom? And if was to repent so they he would not have any guilt they would still throw him** into the sea.

Verse 13

Why do they now, at this point in the story, **try to row back to the dry land? Why didn't they do this immediately** when the storm first hit?

Chapter Two

Verses 3–11

In this prayer comes words are doubled and multiplied. What is written in verses 4 and 5 is repeated in verses 6 and 7 and appears a third time in verse 8. And the **difficult problem of why the entire text of the prayer appears in the past tense has already been explained by Rabbi Abraham Ibn Ezra.**

11. *"Vayomru alav mah na'aseh lecha, And they said to him, "What should we do with you?"* **They asked him, if he wanted to turn in repentance to accept upon himself** the mission **to go to Nineveh. Perhaps there will be to them** the opportunity **to remedy** the situation by their hands **that they will repent with him and travel to the harbor which leads to Nineveh or they will return him to the Land of Israel** from which he would travel to Nineveh. **And as a result** *"vayishtok hayam mei'alinu, the sea will grow quiet from upon us."*

12. *"Vayomeir aleihem sauni vahatiluni el hayam, And he said to them, "Pick me up and throw me into the sea."* **I want to say,** that Jonah said, "I do not want to repent and go to Nineveh. This storm is not to bring me back to my land or to Nineveh. For this storm came to punish me for the transgression of rebelling against the mouth of the Eternal. And this *'yodei'ah ani, I know'* clearly that the storm is not for you as**

a punishment for what you have done by bringing me to Tarshsish for this is not the way the Eternal works. Only *"b'sheli hasaar hagadol hazeh aleichem, because of me this great storm is upon you"* to punish me alone, not because of you. When I sink into the sea, the sea will become quiet around you.

13. *"Vayacht'ru ha'anashim, And the men rowed hard."* They wanted to try this, in that they rowed hard *"l'hahsiv el hayabasha, to return to the dry land"* to travel in return to Jaffa. If the main intention of the Eternal was to return him to his land from which he had fled, would it not appear to be reasonable to the sailors that they would be able to return to dry land to bring the fugitive back to his master. *"V'lo yachlu ki hayam holeich v'sa'ar, And they were able because the sea going and storming."* After Jonah did not turn in repentance, the storm did not rise to silence.

14. *"Vayikru v'chulei el YHVH vayomru al-na novda benefesh ha'ish hazeh, And they called to The Eternal saying do not destroy us on account of this man."* They want to say that if we had not thrown him into the sea would we not have been destroyed because of the soul of this man. That on account of his sinful soul we would all be lost. And that is not what we deserve. And if we throw him into the sea, on this side we ask *"v'al titein aleinu dam naki, do not count it as innocent blood,"* to punish us for his drowning (for they are also obligated to punishment from the heavens and they could receive punishment from human beings who punish the murderer, as is written, "And also on the nation which they serve I will bring judgment" (Gen 15:14). And as it says, "God let him fall into his hand" (Exod 21:13) *"vata YHVH ka'asher chafatzta asit, for you are the Eternal as you desired you have acted."* They, the sailors, want to say to God that this act of causing Jonah's death by throwing him into the sea is not connected with us but only with You, for You brought this storm and You wanted to drown him in the sea and You did as You wished. For we are forced to do this, for if we do not throw him into the sea we will all drown. Therefore this deed is connected to You and not to us.

15. *"Vayisu et-Yonah vay'tiluhu el-hayam, And they lifted Jonah up and lowered him into the sea.* Our sages explained that at the beginning they lowered part of his body in the water and the sea grew quiet and when they lifted him up out of the water it returned to storming. And this is hinted at in what is written *"vay'tiluhu el-hayam, and lowered him into*

the sea." The text uses the word "lowered" it does not say that **they immediately threw him in. At the beginning they carried him in their hands and they performed several trials and they saw that when they lowered him the sea stood** quietly **from its anger. And it is the case that they would not have lowered him into the water with out certainty** that the storm was because of him **for they had many tests: the** unique **character of the storm that it only affected this ship, from the many castings of the lots which all fell on Jonah, from his own announcement, and from the final experience that each time that they lowered him into the sea it stood** quiet **from its storming.**

Chapter Two

1. **"Vayaman YHVH dag gadol, And the Eternal summoned a large fish."** The Eternal invited a big fish to this place that swallowed him whole and did not break his bones. And this is known that it is impossible for a man to live in the belly of the fish even or one hour. For a man has to breathe cold air from the outside. However he had already decreed death upon him, this can be thought of as a second birth. For the Eternal has caused the sinner to drown, to be created and maintained for nine months in the belly of his mother without breathing air. Like Rabbi Yitzhak Abarbanel wrote this is one of the wonders created like miracle of Chanania, Mishael, and Azariah,** referred to by their Chaldean names Shadrach, Meshach, and Abed-Nego in the third chapter of Daniel, **in fiery furnace** (Dan 3:19–30) **and other similar** miracles.

2. **"Vayitpalei meimei hadagah, And he prayed from the belly of the fishette."** Our sages said that at first he was in the belly of a male fish and afterwards it spewed him out and a female fish swallowed him. And it was narrow there,** in the belly of the female fish, **because of the eggs in her belly** so Jonah was moved to pray. In the belly of the male fish there been a lot of room so he was not moved to pray (Pirke D'Rabbi Eliezer 10). **And in truth the noun "dag, fish," includes both the male and the female and the noun "daga, fishette," is a collective noun. And this is like "v'hadaga asher b'yaor meita, and the fish in the Nile died"** (Exod 7:21). *Daga* here cannot refer to female fish for certainly all the fish in the Nile died during the first plague. **And from what is written "meimei hadagah, from the belly of the fishette"** it is taught that it was from the belly of a collective of

many fish. And from this it can be clarified that it was a female fish at the time of reproducing that already one would find in one fish multitudes of eggs that they thought of as if they already are many fish. And their, the sages of Pirke D'Rabbi Eliezer, words are true.

3. "*Vayomeir karati, And he said I called.*" This prayer is divided into three parts. (Part one) It tells the story of the moment he was thrown into the sea and thus gave up hope of living. But when the fish swallowed him and he remained alive in its belly he saw that he had been raise up by a miracle and a wonder and that he would live. (Part two) After he is vomited by sent male fish the again into deep depths he despaired again and when the female fish swallowed him again be believes he will live. (Part three) The moment he is in the narrow belly of the female fish at the time he accepts upon himself to heed the Eternal and to go to Nineveh according to the word of the Eternal.

And he says at the beginning in a general way "*Karati mitzara el YHVH va'aneini, I called to the Eternal from my distress and he answered me.*" For the two times that he was in the sea and called to the Eternal who answered him through the means of the male fish and the female fish who swallowed him.

And now "*mibeten Sheol shivati, from the belly of Sheol I cried out.*" The belly of the female fish is described as Sheol, ready to destroy him.

And he confidently proclaims that "*shamata b'koli, you heard my voice.*" And brought me out fully alive.

4. "*Vatashlicheini, You cast me*" (Part One of Jonah's prayer). It begins to explain what is written "*Karati mitzara el YHVH, I called to the Eternal from my distress.*" For at first You sent me "*m'tzula bilvav yamim, into the depths, into the heart of the seas.*" This refers to what happened when they threw him from the ship into the sea.

"*V'nahar y'sov'veini, And the river swirled around me.*" There a river enters the water that is pulling him. And it is divided from the sea, the water has been standing innocently. But as the storm stirs up the sea that came from the depths, from the sea itself, he felt a surging downward current that is described as a river. For then the water did not stand quietly it pulled in a circle around him, around him, around and around.

And thus "*kol mishbarecha v'galecha alai avaru, all your breakers and waves swept over me.*" He did not float on the waves like the story of

Rabbi Akiva. He simply fell into the depths of the sea, a place where the water flows downward. And the waves pass over him from above.

5. "*Va'ani amarti, I said*" Malbim explains that Jonah did not actually speak the words which follow. It means to say, I thought that "*nigrashti mineged einecha, I was driven from your sight.*" And in that I saw the miracle that the fish swallowed me and I remained alive. I saw that your eyes still watch over me. And because of that I knew that "*osif od l'habit el-heichal kodshecha, I will again see your holy temple.*"

6. "*Afafuni, Encompassed me.*" (Part Two of Jonah's prayer.) After the male fish spewed me back into the sea then "*afafuni mayim ad nefesh, the water encompassed me to the soul.*" Not the water in the area of the sea from the beginning but "*t'hom y'sov'veini, the depths swirled around me.*" For the male fish was with him in the depths of the sea and there it spewed him. The sea of "*suf, reeds*" for the water above from the depths is called *suf*, reeds (for the fish took him by the way of the Sea of Reeds and from there taking him to Nineveh. And it was "*chavush l'roshi, tangled to my head.*" For the sea was above his head after he was in the great depths.

7. "*L'kitzvei harim yarad'ti, To bases of the mountains I descended.*" That I was in the deep of the depth under the mountains. For the mountains cover the depths from above until "*ha'aretz, the land*" which covers the depths which are under the land. And to there "*b'richeha va'adi l'olam, its bars against me forever.*" So that it would not be possible for Jonah to float on the water because above it over him was land. The depths were closed by the land as if with bars and doors. And in all of this "*vataal mishachat chayai, and you lifted my life from the pit.*" Malbim connect this phrase with a specific part of the narrative. That he was swallowed by the female fish and kept alive a second time. And this explains by what is written in verse three "*Karati mitzara el YHVH va'aneini, I called to the Eternal from my distress and he answered me.*" The second fish is God's answer to Jonah's prayer.

8. "*B'hitateif, in the wrapped*" (Part Three of Jonah's prayer). This explains what is written in the second half of verse three "*mibeten Sheol shivati, from the belly of Sheol I cried out.*" For now "*b'hitateif alai nafshi, my soul is wrapped around me.*" He was close to death in the belly of the female fish because of the pressure of the embryos that were in her belly. "*Et YHVH zacharti, The Eternal I remembered.*" And now I remembered

to pray and to turn in repentance, to promise that I will fulfill the word of the Eternal. *"V'tavo eilecha tifilati el heichal kodshecha, That my prayer came to You, to Your holy Temple."* Our sages said that he was in the depths of the sea under Mount Zion upon which stood the Temple. About this the text in verse seven says, *"l'kitzvei harim yarad'ti, to bases of the mountains I descended."* And you heard my prayer from your Holy Temple.

9. *"M'shamrim, zealously guarding."* Now that he has accepted upon himself the mission to go to Nineveh to rebuke them according to the word of the Eternal, he said to himself words of comfort, "Are not the people of Nineveh *'m'shamrim chavlei shav, zealously guarding worthless futilities'* and believers in idols?" And so it is possible *"chasdam ya'azovu, they will forsake their kindness."* That they will forsake their idol worship (in the use of the word *chesed* as "disgrace," as in Leviticus 20:17). But certainly they will not repent of the sin of idolatry which is in their hands. Or it could say that they will repent for the moment but afterwards return to their disgrace and for a second time be deserving of destruction.

10. *"Va'ani, And I"* so that *"ezb'cha-lach, I will bring sacrifices to you"* *"b'kol toda, with a voice of thanksgiving."* Malbim present the words of the verse in a new sequence. For with four sacrifices those "who go down to the sea in ships" (Ps 107:23) have to give thanks to God. This means to say I will bring a Thanksgiving Offering and thank you for your kindness.

And also *"asher nadarti ashaleima, what I have vowed I will fulfill"* to go to Nineveh. And what I feared, that the King of Assyria will bring evil upon Israel, so therefore to express his concern that God should prevent this from happening he says, *"yeshuata laYHVH, for salvation is the Eternal's."* I hope that the Eternal will redeem Israel from all her difficulties.

11. *"Vayomeir YHVH ladag, And the Eternal spoke to the fish."* He awoke the spirit of the fish to take him to the shore of the sea and to spew him onto dry land. And our sages said in Pirke D'Rebbi Eliezer that the fish took him 965 *parasot* (3,860 miles). And it remembers the words of the Eternal and says, *"Vayomeir YHVH ladag vayakei et-Yonah, And the Eternal spoke to the fish and it spewed Jonah."* For three days he was there in the belly of the fish.

Chapter Three

1. *Vay'hi davar YHVH el Yonah sheinit, And the word of the Eternal came to Jonah a second time."* **Rabbi Yitzchak Abarbanel commented about what our sages wrote that this was the second time He spoke with him and not the third.** The question is, did the events described here in the book of Jonah take place before or after the event concerning Jonah mentioned in 2 Kings 14:25? If the events in 2 Kings happened first should not this verse read "And the Eternal spoke to Jonah a third time?" **This is proven by what is written in Seder Olam that Jonah served Yehu in the year 3062 from the creation of the world. And that was until Zacharia who ruled in 3164. And there was from the day that he began his prophecy 102 years. And we do not find another prophecy from him during this time. For the two prophecies** are two prophecies **that he prophesied on Nineveh. From this we knew that prophecy from him ceased since then. For was he suitable to do so,** to prophecy, **after he forsook prophesy and did not want to fulfill the word of the Eternal?**

It is amazing that he contradicts himself as it is written after this it is proven that the prophecy of Jonah on Nineveh was six years before the destruction of Samaria, that this was in the days of Hosea ben Ela, the last King of Israel, **and this was after he prophesied ten years in the days of Menachem ben Gadi,** a king of Israel, **two years in the days of Pakchiya his son,** a king of Israel, **twenty years in the days of Pekach,** a king of Israel, **and three** years in the days of **Hosea. And so the entire length of his prophesying was 137 years** (See 2 Kgs 15–17). **And also the prophecy of Nineveh was not at the end of his days.**

How can a prophet see what the Eternal has not spoken to him before this incident saying that in the future he will take prophecy from him. And in addition amazingly we read **in the book of Nahum that forty years after the time that Jonah prophesied was the destruction of Samaria. And also connected to this, eighty years the destruction of Nineveh. And was there not from the destruction of Samaria to the destruction of Nineveh, that was in the fourth year of Yehoyakim, 114 years? And this also contradicts what is written that the prophecy of Jonah was six years before the destruction of Samaria.**

Questions

Verse 2

Why is there a change this time from the language which God uses in 1:2 **as** here it says, *"U'kra aleha et-hakria asher anochi doveir eilecha, Proclaim upon it the proclamation that I will speak to you."* **And it does not use the language that was used the first time** that God called Jonah in chapter one?

Verse 4

Why does Jonah refrain from proclaiming until he has walked into the city *"mahalach yom echad, a one day's walk?"*

2. *"Kum leich, Get up and go."* This time since He had already issued their judgment, He does nor say, *"kee alta ra'atam l'fanai, for their evil has arisen before me"* as He does in 1:2. **He only sends him on the way to Nineveh for it is known to them what has been decreed concerning them, that Nineveh will be overturned in forty more days.**

3. *"Vayakom vayeilech el Nineveh k'davar YHVH, And he got up and went to Nineveh in accordance with the word of the Eternal."* **Because in the first time God commanded him to pronounce to them words of rebuke which would turn them from their sins. This time God commanded him to deliver the judgment which had been decreed concerning them. And he was in doubt if he should also fulfill the first words and make known to them their designation for overturning and also rebuke them for their sins? This explains that now he would only proclaim what the Eternal spoke to him now, for after He, God, told him, Jonah, the judgment he, Jonah, thought that repentance would no longer be effective for them and that God's first pronouncement** of rebuke **had been canceled.**

"Nineveh heita ir gediola Leilohim, Nineveh was a great city to God." It was connected to God because of its size, like "an intense flame of God" (Song 8:6). Or I could say that it was important in the eyes of God as a great city previously. Therefore the end came to it for its sin.

4. *"Vayachal Yonah lavo va'ir mahalach yom echad, And Jonah began to come into the city a one day's walk."* For he was in doubt when the time of

forty days would begin after he was walking three days. And if he would proclaim immediately on the first day it would cause the residents of the edge of the city to think count the forty days from that day. And the residents on the other edge of the city would begin to count from the third day for the text tells us that it is a three day walk across the city. Therefore, he refrained from proclaiming until he had walked one day. And he proclaimed on the second day. And he thought from the same day to begin the accounting that it is the middle day.

"*Vayikra vayomeir od arba'im yom, And he proclaimed saying forty days more.*" Not including this day. That it is forty days with the last day. And in this his prophecy would be fulfilled in any case. Rabbi Yitzchak Abarbanel thought that in this case there are many ways of understanding how could the prophecy of Jonah not be literally fulfilled? He explained what is written, "*v'Nineveh nehpachet, and Nineveh will be over turned*" means that either it turned itself in its deeds and preparations from evil to good or literally was turned over in destruction. Also it is written that the word is fulfilled by understanding "*arba'im yom, forty days*" to refer to forty years. And taking into account the use of the word "*od, another*" it can be counted as eighty. I want to say that "*od, another*" and forty combine to be 120. That 120 years after this Nineveh is destroyed by Nebuchadnezzar. And I have already written that there is a discrepancy in these calculations. In truth there is no need for all of this. The proclamation was known by God to be conditional. If they would not repent from their evil ways, Nineveh would be over turned. Like what is written "If at any time I declare concerning a nation or a kingdom that I will pluck up or destroy it and if that nation, concerning which I have spoken, turns from its evil, I will repent of the evil that I intended to do to it" (Jer 18:7–8).

And why is it asked was it necessary for Jonah to explain that Nineveh would be destroyed if they did not turn in repentance. This is not a difficulty for they already knew this from the fact that God sent a prophet to warn them. For if it was a decree of destruction without the possibility of change, there would have been no need to announce it through a prophet. For a prophet is not sent except to turn the people in repentance and therefore cancel the decree. And in truth it was apparent to Jonah himself to do this. For thus he was commanded the first time God spoke to him as described in chapter one. Only he did not fulfill all the words. He did not declare anything except the decree that came to

him in the second pronouncement from God described here in chapter three. **And it was his will that they would** continue to **go astray and not repent.**

And if we want to say following the words of Rabbi Yitzhak Abarbanel that the prophecy was fulfilled after many **years, we can say that the mission of Jonah was in the days of** King **Menachem ben Gadi** of Israel. **And the decree** of destruction **of the Kingdom of Assyria was fulfilled to some extent in the fifteenth year of** the reign of **Hezekiah, that was forty years after the mission of Jonah, that an angel of the Eternal overturned the camp of Assyria, that Nineveh was the capital of the kingdom.** The Assyrian army had laid siege to Jerusalem. God, through an angel, sent a plague on the Assyrian army causing them to break off the siege and return to Assyria (2 Kgs 20:35–36). **And** after he returned to Nineveh **the sons of the King** Sennacherib **struck him the sword. And this fulfilled the promise** of Jonah **to some extent.**

5. ***"Vaya'aminu anshei Nineveh Beilohim, And the people of Nineveh believed in God."*** **And it is notable that they believed immediately and they did not ask for a sign or a miracle. And immediately they began to pray through the means that they put on sackcloth to fast and be humble. And the nation was not roused to repentance because it did not occur to them that they were sinners because Jonah had not informed of this. This is how it appears to me.**

6. ***"Vayigah, And it reached."*** **But at the moment the word reached the king, for it also roused him, to humble himself so "*vayakam mikiso vayaveir aderet malchuto*** (*adarto* not *aderet malchuto* in the actual Jonah text) ***meialav, He removes his royal robe from upon himself."*** **And replaces it, *"vay'chas sak, and he covers himself with sackcloth."*** **And in place of his throne, *"vayeishev al-haefer, And he sat on the ashes."***

7. ***"Vayazeik, And it was proclaimed."*** **And in addition to this, he commanded that it be proclaimed *"mita'am hamelech u'g'dolav, from the counsel of the king and his nobles"*** **and his advisors came forth this proclamation saying, *"ha'adam v'hab'heima, the person and the animal*** (**referring to an animal which is to be found in a person's house)** ***al yitamu m'uma, shall not taste anything." "Habakar v'hatzon, The cattle and the sheep"*** **that are grazing in the field *"al yiru, shall not graze"*** **and all of them**—those animals in the homes and those in the fields—***"mayim al yishtu, shall not drink water."***

8. *"Vayitcasu, And they shall cover themselves."* Also in the covering with sackcloth the animals are included. And in addition, the animals participated in the **prayer that** it says, *"vayik'ru el-Elohim b'chazaka, they cried out to God mightily."* And in **repentance** *"Yashuvu kol* [*kol* does not occur in the text of Jonah] *ish midarko hara'a umin hechamas, Every person turned from his evil way and from the robbery."* **For from the robbery the confession and the contrition have no effect until the robber returns what he has to its owner.**

9. *"Mi yodei'ah yashuv, Who knows he will repent."* **That every one will repent from the sin that they know. And concerning that they are obligated to repent for their hidden sins as well, and like they are contrite, thus** *"v'nicham Haelohim, and God repented."* **From the decree** of destruction, **and by this He reassured them that** *"sh'yashuv* [in the actual text the word is *shav* and it follows the word *Elohim*] *Haelohim meicharon apo, God will repent from his burning anger."* **Because from** the message that **was sent to them by the prophet they understood that they had the possibility to repair** their situation **through repentance.**

10. *"Vayar Haelohim et-ma'aseihem, And God saw their deeds."* **It means to say that at the beginning, the repentance of the people of Nineveh was only contrition but they did not turn in deed to repair the transgressing sin through deed. But after the command of the king, God saw all their deeds as repentance. For they repented through their deeds by returning what they had stolen and** everything they acquired through **exploitive activity. And therefore** *"vay'nachem Haelohim al-hara'a, and God repented from the evil."* **And they originally did not repent of the sin of robbery and not of the** sin of idolatry, **nevertheless after the proclamation of the decree they repented for** the sin of robbery **and that repaired their situation.**

   "Lo asa et hara'a, And He did not do the evil." [While this phrase is consistent with the sense of verse 10, these words do not appear in this sequence in the verse.] This means to say that if the evil was prepared to come upon them in nature despite the pressure that was coming on them. Also since they still practiced idolatry so they were under the pressure. The Eternal does not violate nature for those who practice idolatry. But after the natural event passed over them there would not be future evil coming upon them. Only if the Eternal determines to do evil as punishment of supervision, for when they repented for the sin of robbery He

did not perform an act of punishment for their sins. **And He set aside** His intention **to control them through** acts of **nature and pressure.**

Questions

Verses 1 to 3

What is this grief of Jonah? Did he not know of this possible out come? **For this purpose the Eternal sent him, in order to turn them to repentance so that He could cancel the decree** of destruction.

   And from this it is written *"Halo-zeh d'vari ad-heyoti al-adamati, Was this not my words when I was still in my land?"* **What is** the meaning of **this? Did he not** by causing the Ninevites to repent **fulfill his mission in a better way? In turning away from** sin **the result of his mission of the prophet. If the people had not repented one could say as a result of this** "I said, 'I have labored in vain, I have spent my strength for nothing and vanity" (Isa 49:4). **And should he not rejoice that so many** people **repented from sin?**

Verse 4

From what is written, *"Haheiteiv chara lach, Does this deeply grieve you?"* **This is a question that does not have a general meaning, and Jonah does not respond to it with a word like** he does **when he says after this** in verse 9 *"Haheiteiv chara li ad mavet, I am deeply grieved to the point of death."*

Verse 5

Why does he sit to the east of the city what will be in the city? Does he not already know that the Eternal repented from the evil?

Verses 6 to 11

What is this incident of the kikayon, and the rebuke with which the Eternal rebukes him?

Chapter Four

1. *"Vayeira el Yonah, This displeased Jonah."* **Rabbi Yitzchak Abarbanel explains the evil which is referred to here is an illness. In sorrow of his heart he falls ill and he ask for death. And this is because Jonah thought that the decree would not be canceled from over them until they repented in faith and knowledge with deeds. And they did not repent only from their deeds, as it is written** in 3:10 *"vayar Haelohim et-ma'aseihem, and God saw their deeds."* God saw **that they repented** from their sins **and still held fast to idolatry. Nevertheless, the Eternal forgave** the Ninevites and canceled **the evil** decree of destruction. **And from this he understood that the Eternal will maintain them for they are prepared to be "a rod of his anger" upon Israel and this grieved him. And he explains that it grieved him that he was the reason they will remain a staff to bring harm upon Israel despite the fact that they remain idolaters.**

2. *"Halo zeh d'vari, Was this not my word."* **He wants to say that when I was on my land, in the Land of Israel, before I went to Nineveh this was my word the you would forgive Nineveh. He wants to say I knew then that it was not in Your thoughts to bring upon them the evil. You forgave them immediately at the time of the decree from the side of mercy and patience even if they would not perform repentance in a proper way. Behold they did not perform repentance for the sin of idolatry nevertheless You did not bring upon them the evil** of destruction **because you had already forgiven them their evil thus for a small improvement** in their behavior **you cancelled the decree.**

   "Al-kein kidamti livroach Tarshisha, Therefore I hasten to flee towards Tarshish." **He wants to say that I did not flee because I thought that they would perform a proper repentance. In that case I would not have refused to go on a mission to turn sinners from their path.** I refused to go **only because I knew that they would remain worshippers of idols and you would not destroy them. For that** reason **I did not want to go on the mission.**

3. *"Vata YHVH, And now Eternal."* **After they have not performed a full repentance and nevertheless they remain** alive. **They will be "a rod of punishment" for Israel, so take my life, in that I have caused this to** happen.

4. *"Vayomeir YHVH haheiteiv chara lach, And the Eternal said, 'Are you deeply grieved?"* He (God) said to him (Jonah), "Why are you deeply grieved? Is it because they will think of you as a false prophet because your prophecy was not fulfilled? Because if you had prophesied about a good thing and that prophecy was not fulfilled then the reason for your anger would be clear. For if the prophecy was for good and it was not fulfilled, that would have strengthened the belief that the prophet was a false prophet. For the positive promise that comes through the prophet must be fulfilled in any case, even if the people do evil in their deeds. From what is written here concerning an evil assembly, if they turn in repentance the decree is cancelled and the prophet did not speak falsely in this prophecy as is clarified in the words of the prophet Jeremiah to Hanaya ben Azur in Jeremiah 28.

5. *"Vayeishev . . . ad asher yireh ma y'hiye ba'ir, And he sat . . . until he would see what would happen in the city."* For he thought that even though God had cancelled the decree and there would not be a general destruction of the city nonetheless it was impossible that there would not be some impressive event. There would be some evil in the city like the incident of the golden calf, as is written, "And the Eternal repented of the evil which he thought to do to his people" (Exod 32:14); nonetheless, "And the Eternal sent a plague upon the people that had made the calf" (Exod 32:35). Earlier in verse 10, God had told Moses, "my anger burns hot against them and I will consume them." In verse 14 God decides not to destroy them but in verse 35 still punishes them. This creates Jonah's expectation that even though God has decided not to destroy Nineveh there would still be a serious punishment. This is the explanation of Rabbi Yitzhak Abarbanel.

6. *"Vayaman YHVH kikayon, And the Eternal summoned a kikayon plant."* For the shade of the booth did not protect him very much from the sun. As is written, "He sat under it in the shade" (4:5). It should be clarified that there was not shade in the entire booth for the walls of the booth were not covered except for the side the where the sun shone. And in the he had to sit under the eastern wall. And in the middle of the day there was no shade at all. The kikayon provided shade from above on his head to protect him. For his head was vulnerable to be injured by the heat of the sun.

"Vayismach Yonah al-hakikayon, And Jonah rejoiced over the ki-kayon." For Jonah concluded from this that the Eternal wanted him to sit east of the city, for He would bring there some bad thing on the city. He stopped him so that he would see the evil ones receive their recompense.

7. *"Vatach et-hakikayon, And in attacked the kikayon."* It cut it below, at its roots, and in this way it "withered."

8. *"Ruach kadim charishit, a stifling eastern wind."* The word *charishit* is not usually used to describe the wind. Malbim connects it with the word *charash*, deaf. **It deafens the ears with great bending. It is a very hot wind.**

9. *"Haheiteiv chara-l'cha al-hakikayon, You grieve deeply for the kikay-on."* God **asks him for this is a good thing. For the reason that kikayon is a modest thing and it grieves you.**

"Vayomeir heiteiv li, And he said, 'I am deeply grieved.'" He wants to say, **"It grieves me** *'ad mavet, to death."* Because of the absence of the kikayon I am going to die." For its absence **gave birth to a fever kindled by the heat. He grew faint and it drew him close to gates of death.**

10. *"Vayomeir YHVH ata chasata al-hakikayn, And the Eternal said, 'You are took pity on the Kikayon.'"* It is clear to me that there is a difference between *chusa*, pity, and other similar words like *chamal*, compassion, and *racham*, mercy. For *chusa* is in the category of his need like, "Do not *tachos eineichem*, literally pity with your eyes, **pay attention to your belongings"** (Gen 45:20). Joseph tells his brothers that they should not bring their belongings to Egypt because he will provide for them. Here the text **wants to say that you had pity on the kikayon because you needed it to provide you with shade. In this way there is nothing to appeal in you to become sad. Not in the category that you planted it or caused it to grow. For concerning this, the text says, "you did not labor for it." It is the way of laborer to take pity on the work of his hands and not because the thing itself was valuable and viable. For "in a night it was and in a night it vanished." It was a withered sprout and there was not much to it.**

11. *"Va'ani lo achos al-Nineveh, And should I not take pity on Nineveh?"* **For they are works of my hand. And it is a valuable thing. For it is an** *"ir gedola, A big city."* **For also there are many idolaters there. For it has** *"harbei mishtaim-esrei ribo adam asher lo-yada bein-y'mino lismolo, more than one hundred and twenty thousand persons who do not know*

their right hand from their left." For they do not have the knowledge to distinguish between the worship of special God represented by the right hand. As is written, "From his right hand will not move; I am always with you, you held my right hand" (Ps 73:23). And the worship of the left which is worship of nature and array of heavenly bodies which are connected to the left side. And they should not be punished because of their lack of knowledge. And there are also many animals. If a man sins, what is the sin of the animal? And from this we receive an answer also concerning the punishment of Israel. For they already learned the difference between right and left. For they received the knowledge of God and the true faith. And they are appropriately punished for any idolatrous worship they perform. And the people of Nineveh are not punished for this.

6 Divrei Simcha

INTRODUCTION TO DIVREI SIMCHA

AFTER CENTURIES OF COMMENTARY, there is still more to be said about the book of Jonah. Each of the previous commentators wrote from the context of their time and place. I bring a twenty-first century American perspective. Also I found some questions which did not catch the eyes of the earlier commentators. For example, in 1:12, why does Jonah need the sailors to throw him into the sea? Why does he not simply jump? None of the classic commentators discuss this issue.

In my comments I do not restate quotations from the Midrash or focus on grammatical issues. Rather, I explore character and narrative. I describe the relationship of this text to other biblical texts and the inner connectedness of this text. We will see that the author of Jonah often makes use of phrases from other biblical books.

The early commentators assumed that their readers would be engaging the biblical text in Hebrew. I point out the subtleties of the Hebrew which a person who reads the text only in English misses.

The introduction to the other commentators contained biographical background. Therefore, let me say a few words about myself. Born in 1950, I am a graduate of the University of Minnesota and the Hebrew Union College. Since 1981 I have served as rabbi of Congregation Etz Chaim in the far western suburbs of Chicago. I teach as an adjunct at Elmhurst College and at Wheaton College.

DIVREI SIMCHA

Chapter One

1. ***"Vayahi d'var YHVH el Yonah ben Amittai, The word of the Eternal came to Jonah the son of Amittai."*** The text does not say that the Eternal spoke to Jonah. This is typical of God's contact with the prophets. In the Torah, God "speaks, *v'ydabeir*" or "says, *vayomer*" to Moses and others. In the historic books of Samuel and Kings, God "says, *vayomer*" In the books of the Prophets the words of the Eternal "come, *vayahi*" to the prophets. Or the prophets have a vision, *hazon*, as in Isaiah and Obadiah.

   Yonah ben Amittai A person who does not know Hebrew will miss a full understanding of the prophet's name. Jonah's name, Yonah, appears in the Tanach in a few ways. In Jeremiah 25:38, 46:16, 50:16 and in Zephaniah 3:1 its meaning is unclear. It may refer to oppression. In various places, most famously in Genesis 8, it means dove. In that story Noah sends the dove three times. Once it comes back with nothing. The second time it comes back with a "freshly plucked olive leaf." The third time it does not return. The dove represents the possibility of a new beginning. The dove returns from its first venture, having failed to find any evidence of the possibility of leaving the ark. The dove succeeds on its second try. Our Yonah also succeeds only on his second try.

   Both stories involve a group of people who have become so evil that God decides to destroy them. Both stories involve trips over the water in boats. Boats do not play a role in many Hebrew Bible stories. The other prominent example is the basket into which Yocheved places Moses in the Nile; this is also a redemption story.

   Ammitai is derived from *emet*, which means truth. Hence, Jonah is the son of truth. Is Jonah actually a person of truth? He only reveals his story to the sailors when the lot falls on him. Generally he hides from the truth or denies the truth. Ben Ammitai is an ironic name for Jonah.

2. ***"Ha'ir hagedola,"*** literally, that large city or that great city. In this context understand it means "prominent city." For Nineveh was the capital of the Assyrian Empire.

   "Ukra Aleha, Proclaim over it." God instructs Jonah to "proclaim over it" but does not tell Jonah what to say. Jonah clearly understands the type of message God would want him to convey. He knows that it will be a message that the Ninevites would not like to hear.

"*Kee-alta ra'atam l'fanai, For their evil has risen before my face.*" God maintains a distance from human affairs. Every day, everywhere people commit evil acts. But the evil of the Ninevites has risen to such an extreme level so that their evil was in God's face. The extent of the evil must have been deep and wide. The individuals must have been committing act of serious evil and the entire population must have been participating. In Genesis 18:32 God assures Abraham that if there exist 10 righteous people in Sodom, God will not destroy the city. God will not destroy the righteous together with the wicked. So we can conclude that all the people of Nineveh were engaging in wickedness.

3. "*Vayakom Yonah livroach, And Jonah arose to flee.*" Many of the prophets, beginning with Moses, express to God their feeling of inadequacy for the job, but Jonah is the only one who flees.

The prophet Amos explains that when God places words of prophecy within a person's mouth, that person must prophesy. The fourth chapter of the book of Amos begins with a series of eight "if . . . then" statements: i.e., "Does the lion roar in the forest when it has no prey?" This series of phrases leads to verse 8 "The Lord God has spoken, who can but prophesy." Amos argues that to prophesy or not to prophesy is not a question. Jonah, alone among the prophets of Israel and Judah, opposes Amos' analysis of the prophetic process. Jonah thinks he can avoid prophesying.

Why does Jonah flee? He is afraid. He fears what the Ninevites will do to him. He is not sent merely to any non-Israelite city but rather to the capital of Assyria, the enemy empire. It is as if at the height of the cold war an American would have been sent to Moscow to publicly proclaim its impending fall. He fears for his life.

In 4:2 Jonah offers an after the fact, self-serving explanation of his flight. He argues that he knew God would forgive the Ninevites and not destroy the city. The continuing existence of the city could make Jonah, who announced its destruction, appear to be a false prophet.

Many Jewish commentators try to provide Jonah with a positive motivation for his flight. They argue that Jonah honors "the child over the parent," the child being Israel and the parent God. They reason that Jonah knew that the Ninevites were close to repentance. If he went to Nineveh and prophesied there the Ninevites would repent. This would cause great embarrassment to the Israelites who never repent of their sins despite pleas of numerous prophets. The stubbornly sinful Israelites would appear to be a morally inferior people in contrast to the repentant Ninevites

The medieval Jewish commentators lived at a time when Jews confronted Christian polemics. The book of Jonah was a battleground for this Jewish/Christian debate, with Christians attacking Jonah and Jews defending.

In our time of respect and understanding between religions, we have moved beyond such polemics. We no longer feel the sting of attacks on our religion and therefore do not feel the need to respond defensively. We can look at the story in its own terms and see that the true motivation behind Jonah's flight is fear.

Many people flee in fear to avoid facing difficult situations. Our means of flight from facing the true reality of our lives include psychological defense mechanisms, drugs, and fanatic religion.

"Tarshisha, towards Tarshish." While the Bible refers to Tarshish several times, the location of Tarshish is unknown. Isaiah speaks of the "ships of Tarshish" in four verses: 2:16, 23:1, 23:14, and 60:9. This could be the source for our author's choice of destination for Jonah. Also the author may have chosen this city as Jonah's destination because of the sound of the word. The hard sound of the word Nineveh contrasts to the soft sound of the word Tarshisha.

"Vayeired Yafo, He went down to Jaffa." This is the first step of Jonah's descent. He goes down from the mountains to Yafo, down from land to the ship, down into the hold of the ship, down into sleep, down from the ship into the sea, down from the surface of the sea to the depths of the sea.

In the Bible, encounters with God often take place on mountaintops. God instructs Abraham to offer Isaac as a sacrifice on Mount Moriah. God gives Moses the Torah on Mount Sinai. God instructs Solomon to build the Temple on what we call the Temple Mount. Elijah confronts the prophets of Ba'al at Muchrakah on Mount Carmel. As Jonah descends to the depths of the sea, he moves farther from God.

4. *"V'YHVH heitil ruach gedola, The Eternal sent a great wind."* God does not send the storm while the ship is still in the Jaffa harbor to prevent Jonah from leaving the Land of Israel. God does not want to control Jonah like a puppeteer pulling a puppet's strings. God creates a situation in which Jonah will be forced to make a choice. God wants to see Jonah's response to life threatening danger.

Generally in the biblical miracle stories, God creates situations which allow for events to unfold in a certain way rather than directly completely changing reality. Rather than directly causing the death of the Canaanite soldiers, God causes the sun to stand still over the valley of Ayalon, so that Joshua can complete his defeat of the Canaanites. Rather than lifting the Israelites out of Egypt, God sends plagues to convince Pharaoh to free the Israelites. The Israelites, themselves, have to act to be saved. They must place the blood of the lamb on the doorposts of their homes.

Here God does not pluck Jonah from the ship. God sends a wind and then allows events to unfold.

5. "*Vayiza'aku ish el-elohav vayatilu et-hakeilim asher b'oneya el hayam, And they cried, each man to his own god and they threw the cargo into the sea.*" The sailors took practical steps to save the ship, while they sought supernatural intervention. While the text does not tell us the nationality and religion of the crew, from the phrase, "each to his own god," we can conclude that it was a mixed group.

"*Vayonah Yarad, And Jonah descended.*" From the sequence of the verse one might conclude that Jonah descended into the hold and went to sleep at the height of the storm. I believe that the final section of the verse describes action which took place before the action described in the first half of the verse. Jonah was already asleep in the hold of the ship when the storm began. The phrase should be understood Jonah had descended. In Hebrew there is no separate past perfect form to describe action which had already been completed. Regular past tense verbs are used for this purpose.

"*Vayeiradam, And he slept.*" The world around him is falling apart and Jonah sleeps. Jonah not only flees from God, he flees from the reality of his own life. His desire to escape must be incredibly strong for him to sleep through such a violent storm. When the going gets tough, Jonah takes a nap. We can see a parallel between Jonah's sleeping here and his wishes for death in 4:3 and 4:8. In all three cases Jonah desires to separate himself from the events of his life.

6. "*Rav hachoveil, The chief of those who pull ropes.*" These words describe the captain. This is the only place in the story in which he appears. Verse four spoke of the sailors. Throughout the rest of the chapter the text speaks of "the men" or "they" without distinguishing between the captain and the sailors. The text does not include the name of the captain or any of the sailors. This is typical of biblical narrative in which we learn very little about the secondary characters.

"*K'ra el elohecha, Cry unto your god.*" The captain wants Jonah to pray to his god. It is not that the captain necessarily believes that Jonah's god is particularly powerful. Jonah's prayer would be one more appeal to one more god. All the people on board were each praying to their own god. Facing imminent destruction the sailors did not debate which one of them prayed to the proper god. They embrace religious pluralism under pressure. It is said, that "in fox holes there are no atheists." In this crisis at sea there are no religious triumphalists, all prayers count. One of them might save the ship.

7. "*V'napila goralot v'neida, Let us cast lots and we will know.*" Despite the sailors' prayers the storm continues. Despite the throwing of the cargo overboard, the ship remains in danger. The storm must have been extraordinary because the sailors now turn to trying to identify which of the ship's company is responsible for bringing this storm upon them. They believe that the storm has supernatural origins. Perhaps it was a storm out of season. In the Caribbean, fall is the hurricane season. So this storm could be the Mediterranean version of a spring hurricane.

While we would view the casting of lots as yielding a random result, the text presents the casting of lots as a reliable way of determining truth. Jonah and the sailors accept it without question.

8. "*Hagida-na lanu, Tell us.*" They do not ask Jonah if he is the cause of the storm. They assume that to be true. All the questions seem directed to finding out what he had done to anger God.

"*Ba'asher l'mi hara'ah hazot lanu, In regard to who is this evil upon us?*" The sailors have already identified Jonah as the man responsible for the storm. Now they want to know more about him. They want to know the source of the storm. This question introduces the series of questions which follows.

The sailors do not directly ask Jonah, "What have you done to deserve such a punishment from the Deity?" Rather they ask him about his membership in groups. Perhaps, a particular group to which Jonah belongs, has been cursed by God.

9. "*Vayomeir aleihem Ivri anochi, And he said to them, "I am a Hebrew."*" Jonah responds to the sailors' general concern rather than to all of their specific questions. Jonah skips the question about this profession. He identifies his nationality and moves on to the heart of the matter, his relationship to the Eternal.

"Et hayam v'et hayabasha, The sea and the dry land." Jonah describes God as the One who formed the sea and dry land, rather than the more typical *shamayim v'aretz*, heaven and earth, emphasizing their predicament and the dryness of the land they seek to reach in order to be saved.

The use of this phrase here recalls the only other the biblical use of *yam* and *yabasha* together. In three places—Exodus 14:16, 14:22, and Nehemiah 9:11—the text uses these words to describe the division of the Reed Sea and the saving of the Israelites from the Egyptians. Jonah's use of the phrase hints at his hope that God will save this ship from the storm by returning it to dry land, as God saved the Israelites from the Egyptians.

10. *"Vayiru ha'anashim yirah gedolah, And the men feared a great fear."* In Hebrew, this phrase sounds similar to the phrase which begins chapter four, *"vayira el Yonah ra'ah gedolah*, It was evil to Jonah a great evil." The two phrases describe opposite situations. Here in 1:10 the sailors appropriately fear for their lives. There in 4:1 Jonah inappropriately denounces God for forgiving the Ninevites. The author makes clever use of the similarity in sound of *vayiru* and *vayira*.

"Ki higid lahem, For he had told them." This is an odd sentence. Why does the text refer to "off-stage" comments rather simply including those comments in Jonah's telling of his tale? This last phrase seems added on. Perhaps the original text did not include these three words. A later editor could have read the verse and asked him/herself how did the sailors know the story of Jonah's flight? Rather than rewriting the entire verse the editor added these words to the end of the verse to solve the narrative problem. Alternatively, we can maintain the integrity of the text by describing this phrase as a creative "storytelling technique."

11 *"Mah na'ase lach, What should we do to you?"* The sailors have accepted Jonah's explanation of the source of the storm. The sailors don't ask, "What should we do?" They ask, "What should we do to you?"

12. *"Sa'uni vahatiluni el hayam, Pick me up and throw me into the sea."* Jonah courageously tells the sailors to throw him overboard. He believes this will lead to his death and the survival of the sailors. Jonah has no idea that God will save him. But why do the sailors have to throw him into the sea? Why can't he jump into the sea? Why does he require sailor-assisted suicide?

Two other biblical figures do take their own lives. In 1 Samuel 31, King Saul has been badly wounded by Philistine archers. He is about to be captured by the Philistines. He fears what they will do to him. So in verse 4, "Saul said to his armor bearer, 'Draw your sword and thrust me through with it lest these uncircumcised come and make sport of me.' But his armor bearer would not, for he feared greatly. Therefore Saul took his own sword and fell upon it.'"

Chapter 16 of the book of Judges tells the story of Samson's death. In verse 23, as part on an offering to their god Dagon the Philistines proclaim, "Our god has given Samson our enemy into our hand." The Philistines bring Samson from his cell and make sport of him. In verse 30, Samson prays to God asking for the return of his strength "And Samson said, 'Let me die with the Philistines.' Then he bowed with all his might; and the house fell upon the lords and upon the people who were in it. So the dead were more than he had slain during his life."

Saul does turn to another who does not act quickly. We will see that the sailors also do not act quickly. Like the armor bearer they are reluctant to take a life. Saul and Samson kill themselves. Jonah does not have strength of will of Saul or Samson to take his own life. Jonah plays a more passive role. He has concluded that he must die for the sailors to live but he depends upon them to take his life.

"Ki yodaiah ani, For I know." Jonah now tells the sailors that he knows that this storm is because of him. He now knows that God will not let him go. When did he know this? When he boards the ship and takes refuge in the hold he believes that he can escape. He closes his eyes and goes to sleep. As if playing cosmic peek-a-boo. His eyes are closed so God must not be there. He opens his eyes when the captain awakens him. While he does not admit it to the sailors until the lot falls on him, he sees God's presence in the storm. He knew that this storm was because of him from the moment he woke up. He wakes up from his sleep and from his dream that he can escape God's call.

13. **"L'hashiv el hayabasha, To return to dry land."** The sailors ask Jonah a question, they get an answer but they do not immediately follow Jonah's plan. They are not quick to throw Jonah into the sea. They do not want his blood on their hands. They try once more to overcome the storm through conventional means.

14. ***"Vayikru el YHVH, And they cried unto the Eternal."*** Earlier, in verse 5, each sailor prayed to his own god. Here the sailors do not pray to their own gods rather they pray to the one God of Israel, acknowledging the power of that God. They use the four-letter name of The Eternal in their prayer. They have come to understand that YHVH truly rules the universe.

15. ***"Vayatilu el-hayam, And they threw him into the sea."*** How many sailors throw Jonah into the sea? The text does not say "some of them" It says "they." Throughout this chapter Jonah is in conversation with "they" an undifferentiated group of sailors. I take this "they" to mean that all the sailors participate in throwing Jonah into the sea. In verse 13 the sailors work together to row back to dry land in order to avoid facing this moment of taking Jonah's life. Seeing no alternative, they now share in the responsibility for the act they believe will lead to his death.

Nowhere in this story does the text explain how many sailors were on the ship or how large the ship was. On one hand, maybe the author saw these as unimportant details or on the other hand, maybe the author saw this as information that everybody knew. All the readers in the author's society would know how big a ship is and how large the crew would be. Just as a mid-twentieth century writer would not have needed to describe the size of a Cadillac. All of the author's contemporary readers would have known that it was a large luxury car but future generations might not understand this image.

16. ***"Vayiru ha'anashim yirah gedolah et YHVH, And the men feared a great fear to the Eternal."*** The text repeats this phrase from verse 10 but adds *et YHVH*, to the Eternal. The two uses of this phrase bracket the action, from when the sailors learn of Jonah's misdeed to the resolution of the crisis. The text uses the same words twice but they do not convey the same meaning. There, in verse 10, they express the sailors' fear that the Eternal may cause their death as part of the punishment of Jonah. Here, in verse 16, they express the sailors' awe that the Eternal has saved them from death.

"Vayizb'chu zevach laYHVH, They offer offerings to the Eternal." In contrast to the "each man to his own god" of verse five, here the sailors present an offering to YHVH, the God of the Israelites.

"Vayid'ru nedarim, They vowed vows." Combine with the awe and the offerings of the earlier portions of the verse, these vows should be understood as expressing the sailors' commitment to serving the God of the Israelites.

Chapter Two

1. *"**Dag gadol, A big fish.**"* Despite the use of the words *"dag gadol, big fish"* in the text, many people think of Jonah as having been in the belly of the whale. In Western culture we find references to Jonah "in the belly of the whale." Father Mapple, the preacher in the whalers' church in *Moby Dick*, delivers a sermon in which he refers to Jonah in "the belly of the whale." This image of "the whale" may come from later Christian tradition. Modern English translations of Matthew 12:40 have Jesus speaks of Jonah being in "the belly of a whale" (though Matthew's Greek, quoting from the Septuagint version of Jonah, speaks more generally of a sea monster).

To resolve this conflict in word choice between Jonah and the later Christian tradition we need to ask several questions concerning marine biology and biblical languages.

1. Do whales live in the Mediterranean Sea?

According to World Wild Life Fund, four types of whales live in the Mediterranean Sea: the Fin Whale, the Sperm Whale, the Pilot Whale, and the Beaked Whale. There are also three kinds of dolphin: the Striped Dolphin, the Bottlenose Dolphin, and the Grampus Dolphin.

2. When did people place whales and fish into separate categories?

The earliest extant text making this distinction comes from Aristotle (384 to 322 BCE). He described whales, dolphins, and porpoises as cetaceans and distinguished them from fish: "The dolphin, the whale and all the rest of the cetacea, all that is to say, that are provided with a blow-hole instead of gills, are viviparous. . . . The dolphin has been asleep with his nose above water and when asleep he snores . . ."

3. Were the authors of Jonah and later biblical texts aware of this work of Aristotle?

It is very possible that the authors of biblical texts written after the time Aristotle's ideas had been disseminated would have known that a whale was not a fish.

The prophet Jonah appears in 2 Kings 14:25. That text describes events of the eighth century BCE reign of King Jeroboam. We know for sure that book of Jonah was written later. Scholars see Jonah as a late book in the Bible, written well after the return from Babylonian exile, most likely between 300 BCE and 200 BCE. So the author of Jonah could have been aware of the teaching of Hellenistic science. Also, it is possible that observers in Judea could have independently recognized the difference between fish and water dwelling mammals, which Aristotle describes.

4. If the author of Jonah had wanted to clearly indicate that a whale had swallowed Jonah could he have chosen a different word/s than dag gadol? *Does biblical Hebrew have a word for whale?*

Modern Hebrew uses *tanin* for crocodile. Biblical Hebrew uses it more generally to refer to large water dwelling creatures. In Genesis 1:21, as part of description of the sea creatures, the text says, "God created *taninim gedolim*" generally translated as "great sea monsters." The word *tanin* also is used in Exodus 7:9 to describe the creature into which Aaron turns his staff. It is understood there to be a general term for reptiles. Earlier in Exodus 4:3 at the Burning Bush God instructs Moses concerning turning the staff into a snake. There the text uses the specific word for snake, *nachash*. In Isaiah 27:1 the text speaks of God slaying "the *tanin* which is in the sea," often translated as "dragon."

Another possible word would be Leviatan. The word appears a total of six times in the Hebrew Bible, twice in Isaiah, Psalms, and Job. These books use Leviatan to refer to a large sea creature, perhaps mythical. Isaiah 27:1 and Psalm 74:13–14 use Leviatan in parallel with *tanin*. Psalm 104:26 compares the Leviatan to ships. In Job 40:25–32, God describes to Job the strength and power of the mighty Leviatan. Rabbinic literature uses the word, Leviatan, to refer to a gigantic mythical sea creature, larger than anything ever seen by human beings. Modern Hebrew uses Leviatan to refer to whales.

The author of Jonah could have chosen a *tanin* to swallow Jonah or a Leviatan but in fact chose *dag gadol*.

"Livlo'ah, to swallow him." The text does not speak of what happens to Jonah between the moment the sailors throw him into the sea and the moment that the fish swallows him. It does not explain how long Jonah is in the water before the fish swallows him. As the sailors throw him overboard,

Jonah, certainly believes that he is about to die. As the fish approaches him does he see this as his end or as his salvation?

"*Shlosha yamim ushlosha leilot, Three days and three nights.*" Why does the text need the phrase "and three nights?" Is it not obvious that three days would also include three nights? This is an echo of the Noah story. In Genesis 6:12 it rains "for forty days and forty nights." As the ark protected Noah from drowning in the water of the flood, so the fish will protect Jonah from drowning in the water of the sea.

2 "*Vayitpaleil Yonah, And Jonah prays.*" The text does not clearly tell us when during the three days Jonah begins to pray. The prayer contained in verses 3–10 is a single unit. The ideas move from verse to verse, describing Jonah's descent, his repentance and his devotion to God who saves him. I believe Jonah offered this prayer on the third day, followed immediately by God's instruction to the fish to return him to dry land contained in verse 11. The three days in the belly of the fish recall the three days and nights the Israelites prepared before receiving the Torah in Exodus 19:10–12. The prayers which Jonah offers to God are the words of a confident servant of the Eternal. During these three days in the belly of the fish Jonah changes from a fugitive in flight into a prophet prepared to resume his mission.

"*El- YHVH Elohav, To the Eternal his God.*" Jonah prays to the Eternal his God. Either *YHVH* or *Elohav* would be sufficient to name the object of Jonah's prayer. Why does the text use both terms. This is the first time the book of Jonah uses the expression *Elohav,* his God. YHVH is the name of Deity Jonah addresses. The use of *Elohav* declares that he sees himself in relationship with that Deity. Jonah recognizes that being alive in the belly of the fish is not an accident. He understands that it is a step toward his salvation. Despite Jonah's flight, God remains focused on him. Jonah, now, turns to God.

3. "*Karati mitzarah li el YHVH vayaneini, I called from my distress to the Eternal and He answered me.*" In this prayer many of Jonah's words come from the book of Psalms. The author selects phrases from five psalms which express Jonah thoughts. The author mixes his/her own words with those of psalms to form a coherent prayer. Our author's words sound as if they too could be words of the Psalms. The author assumes that the reader will recognize the lines from Psalms. This technique places Jonah's appeal to God in the context of official well known prayer language.

Throughout the prayer Jonah speaks in the past tense as if his rescue from the sea is complete and he has returned to dry land. This verse would more sensibly be in the present and future tenses, "I call upon the Eternal and He will answer me." Perhaps Jonah speaks in the past tense because he saw himself saved from the moment the fish swallowed him. We could attach theological meaning to the past tense verb forms. We could say that Jonah speaks of God's salvific acts as already completed because of his complete confidence in God. Perhaps the tense of the verbs of the prayer grows out of the fact the verses quoted from the book of Psalms were written in the past tense. The author of Jonah simply maintains the form of the verbs and matches his/her new composition to the Psalms' verbs.

The author bases this line on Psalms 120:1. There, the text reads, *"el YHVH btzarah li karati kayaneini."* Here, our author rearranges the sequence and changes *"btzarah li*, in my distress," to *"mitzarah li*, from my distress" for a reason I will explain below.

"*Mibeten She'ol shivati shamata koli, From the belly of She'ol I cried out, and you heard my voice.*" The author composes the second half of the verse to be in parallel with the first half of the verse. The second part of the verse repeats the ideas of the first half of the verse. Scholars call this synonymous parallelism. This is a very common form of biblical poetry found throughout the wisdom literature, and in poetic sections of biblical narratives such as: Moses' Song of Farewell in Deuteronomy 32:1–43, and the Song of the Sea in Exodus 15:1–18. "From the belly of She'ol I cried out" is parallel to "I called from my distress." "You heard my voice" is parallel to "He answered me." The shift from *"btzarah li*, in my distress" to *"mitzarah li*, from my distress" strengthens the parallel.

"*She'ol*" The depths of the earth, a place far from God. In the belly of the fish Jonah is literally and spiritually in the depths. The Bible often uses the term She'ol to name the destination of those who have died, as in Hannah's prayer in 1 Samuel 2:6. In Psalms 18:6 "the cords of She'ol" are presented as parallel to "the snares of death." Here in our verse, Jonah declares that he was near death, but now he has been rescued from the sea and so he thanks God.

4. **"*Vatashlicheini m'tzula bilvav yamim, v'nahar y'sov'veini, You cast me into the deep, in the heart of the seas, and the river spun around me.*"** In verse 3 Jonah calls to God from the depths, here he acknowledges God as controlling his circumstance. I understand *"v'nahar, river"* to refer the currents and tides of the sea not literally to a river.

"Kol mishbarecha v'galecha alai avru, And all your breakers and your waves passed over me." The second half of this verse comes from the second half of Psalms 42:8 (42:7 in some English translations). The Psalmist is not describing a person in the sea. He/she uses the phrase as part of the phrase poetic image to describe the feelings of a person far from Jerusalem. Our author recognizes that Jonah could say these words. Our author then constructs the first half of our verse to be in parallel with this phrase from Psalms.

5. *"V'ani amarti nigrashti mineged einecha, And I said, 'I was driven from before your eyes.'"* This phrase comes from Psalm 31:23 (22). The phrase in Psalms reads, *"V'ani amarti v'chaftzi nigrazti mineged einech, And I said in my alarm, 'I was cut off from before your eyes.'"* Our author drops *"v'chaftzi, in my alarm"* and replaces *"nigrazti, I was cut off"* with *"nigrashti, I was driven."* Since Jonah does want to express a total break with God, "driven" is better than "cut off." Our author's use of the passive voice may seem curious. For in truth Jonah was not driven from before God, he fled. The verse could have said, *"brachti mineged einecha, I fled from before your eyes."* Our author may have chosen to use the passive form, *"nigrashti, I was driven,"* to maintain the sound and structure of the phrase in Psalms. Or perhaps the passive voice allows Jonah to avoid fully accepting responsibility for his situation.

"Ach osif l'habit el heichal kodshecha, Yet I will again look at your Holy Temple." The second half of this verse expresses confidence that Jonah will not die in the belly of the fish. He believes that being in the fish is a step towards his rescue not simply a temporary reprieve from death. The second half of the verse expresses an idea in contrast to that expressed in the first half of the verse. Scholars call this Antithetic Parallelism.

The second half of this verse marks a turn in the prayer. The first two and a half verses of this prayer describe Jonah's predicament. We might have expected that Jonah would now ask God to intercede on his behalf. But Jonah does not petition God to forgive and save him. Instead, he describes what his relationship with God will be in the future. Jonah seems to assume that he is being saved. From the depths of the sea, he imagines himself ascending to top of the Temple Mount. He will become close to God.

6. *"Afauni mayim ad nefesh, Encompassed me the water to soul."* This is similar to *"ki ba'u mayim ad nefesh, For comes the water to soul"* from Psalms 69:2 (1). From the context of both verses, "my" can be inserted before "soul" to clarify the meaning.

"T'hom y'sov'veini suf chashuv l'roshi, The deep spun around me, weeds wrapped around my head." The image of the weeds raises a narrative problem. How could weeds be causing him trouble if he is the fish? This could be describing his experience after his entrance to the sea and before the fish swallowed him.

7. *"Vata'al mishachat chayai YHVH Elohai, You lifted my life from the pit, Eternal my God."* This phrase again expresses Jonah's confidence in his redemption by the hand of God. The verbs appear in the past tense. Jonah does not seek God's intervention, he praises God's intervention. While Jonah remains in the belly of the fish, we would expect the verbs to be in the future tense. The past tense would seem to be more appropriate for a prayer recited by Jonah after the fish deposits him on dry land.

In the middle of the Song of the Sea, Exodus 15:14–15 the text describes the response of Philistines, the Edomites, the Moabites, and the Canaanites to hearing of God's powerful rescue of the Israelites. The text uses past tense verbs to describe the reaction of these nations to news they could not yet have possibly heard. That poet feels free to speak of future acts as if they have already occurred because he knows what will happen. Because of his confidence in God, Jonah can speak of his return to dry land, as if it had already occurred.

8. *"B'hitateif alai nafshi et YHVH zacharti, vatavo eilecha t'filati el heichal kodshecha, In my soul's wrapping up on me, I remembered the Eternal, and my prayer came to You, to Your Holy Temple."* Jonah proclaims that as he felt himself to be near death his attention turns to God. Jonah then visualizes his appeal reaching God who dwells in the Temple. Here the second part of the verse does not repeat the ideas of the first half, nor does it contrast with the first half, it continues the action. Scholars call this Synthetic parallelism.

9. *"M'shamrim havlei shav, Those who devotedly serve vanities of worthlessness."* This is similar to *"hashomrim havlei shav, Those who serve the vanities of worthlessness"* from Psalms 31:7(6). Our author changes *hashomrim*, in the Kal conjugation, into *m'shamrim*, in the Pi'el conjugation. Pi'el indicates intensive action. My translation of *m'shamrim*, as " those who <u>devotedly</u> serve," expresses the distinction between the Kal and Pi'el forms. This root (Shin, Mem, Reish) appears in the Pi'el only once in the Hebrew Bible, here in our verse. Our author creates this unique usage to describe

the intensity of their devotion to the "vanities of worthlessness." The text does not explicitly tell us to whom this refers. This could be a description of the depth of the sinfulness of the Ninevites.

10. *"B'kol todah, With a voice of thanksgiving."* The prayer concludes with a verse which contains no reference to the dire straits of Jonah's current situation. Rather it expresses Jonah's confidence that his life will continue because of God's saving power.

"Asher nidarti ashaleima, That which I have vowed I will fulfill." What is Jonah's vow? It could be the promises contained in this prayer to bring offerings. More likely it is Jonah's unstated vow to fulfill his mission to Nineveh.

11. *"Vayomeir YHVH ladag, The Eternal spoke to the fish."* God does not speak to Jonah while he is in the belly of the fish. God lets Jonah know that his plea and prayer have been accepted by directing the fish to return Jonah to dry land.

Chapter Three

1. *"Vayhi d'var YHVH el-Yonah sheinit, The word of the Eternal came to Jonah a second time."* God could have sent Jonah home and called another person to be the prophet to the Ninevites. But God gives Jonah a second chance hoping that Jonah has emerged from the fish a new person.

2. *"Kum laich, Arise go."* God does not begin with words of introduction reflecting on Jonah's experiences at sea. God does not tell Jonah, "I going to give you a second chance at this mission." God simply instructs Jonah to go to Nineveh.

3. *"Vayakom Yonah vayeilech, Jonah arose and went."* In Genesis 22:3 we find the same verbs used to describe Abraham's response to God's call to sacrifice Isaac. Jonah acts as a devoted servant of the Eternal.

"Ir gedola Lailohim, A great city to God." In most English translations we do not find the words "to God." These translators see *"Lailohim"* as modifying *"gedola, Great."* The RSV offers "an exceedingly large city." The JPS renders it "an enormously large city." A footnote in the JPS edition indicates that "meaning of the Hebrew [is] uncertain." In the previous verse we read that Nineveh is an *"'ir gedola, a great city."* Here the text repeats

that description and adds *"Lailohim*, to God." Other, clearer words were available to the author if he/she wished to convey "exceedingly large" or "enormously large." I understand this phrase to mean "a city important to God."

   "Mahalach shloshet yamim, A three days walk." Could Nineveh really be so big that it would take a person three days to walk across it? A person could walk across the entire Chicago Metropolitan area in two days. Certainly biblical Nineveh was smaller than the contemporary Chicago Metropolitan area. Earlier commentators solve this problem by suggesting that this phase refers to the entire district not just the city or that it would take three days to explore the city. But I see this is one of several example of exaggeration in the book of Jonah. Others include the severity of the storm, the size of the fish, and the extent of the repentance of the Ninevites.

4. **"Od arba'im yom v'Ninevh neh'pachet, Another forty days and Nineveh shall be overturned."** Jonah does not say to the Ninevites, "<u>If you do not repent</u> Nineveh will be overturned in forty days." He declares, "Nineveh will be overturned in forty days." The Ninevites take it as a warning. Their response indicates that they believe that repentance will save them from destruction. Three times in the Hebrew Bible God announces the intention to destroy populations because of the evil of the inhabitants' behavior: the generation of Noah, Sodom and Gemorrah, and the Ninevites. Only the Ninevites receive a direct verbal warning. The warning serves no purpose except to give them a chance to repent.

   Jonah does not say, "In forty days Nineveh will be destroyed." The text uses the term "*neh'pachet, overturned*" which could be taken as hint at the Ninevites response. They turn over their lives.

5. **"Vayaminu anshei Nineveh beilohim, The people of Nineveh believed in God."** Does this means the Ninevites believed in God's message which Jonah delivered? Or does it mean that the Ninevites had already been believers in God? A pre-existing faith in God would explain why Nineveh merited a visit from a prophet of God and why they respond so quickly and dramatically to Jonah's declaration. This follows Abraham Ibn Ezra's view of the Ninevites as monotheists.

   "Vayikr'u tzom, They declared a fast." The people act before the king issues a royal proclamation. The text describes an immediate grassroots response to Jonah's words.

Fasting is a standard method people in the Hebrew Bible use to seek God's intervention. In 2 Samuel 12:16, King David wants God to heal his gravely ill child. "David fasted . . . and lay on the ground." Often the fast includes large groups of people. In Ezra 8:21, Ezra wants God to protect the people on their journey from Babylonia back to Jerusalem. "So we fasted and besought our God." 2 Chronicles tells of King Jehosaphat of Judah's fear of an attack by the Moabites and the Ammonites. In 20:3 he turns to God. "Then Jehosaphat feared, and set himself to seek the Eternal and proclaimed a fast throughout all Judah."

"Migedolim v'ad ketanim, From the great to the small." Without the benefit of mass media, the word of Jonah's proclamation and the fast spread through out Nineveh. This is another example of our author using grand terms to tell the story.

6. *"Vayigah hadavar el-hamelech Nineveh, And the word reached the king of Nineveh."* Our text could have followed the model of Moses and Aaron directly confronting Pharaoh beginning in Exodus 5:1. Jonah could have appeared before the King of Nineveh to proclaim the city's fate. Rather, Jonah speaks in an unidentified public location in the midst of the general population. The message reaches the King second hand. In the Exodus text Pharaoh was the target of the Eternal's words. Here the Eternal speaks through Jonah to the entire Ninevite population.

"Vayachas sak vayeishev al-ha'eifer, He covered himself *with sackcloth, and sat on ashes."* Sackcloth and ashes often accompany fasting in the biblical period. The prophet Isaiah criticizes the people of his time who fast seeking God's forgiveness but do not forsake their evil ways. In reading his attack on insincere repentance, we can see the connection of sackcloth, ashes and fasting. In 58:5 Isaiah asks on God's behalf, "Is the fast that I choose, a day for a man to humble himself? Is it to bow down his head like a rush, to spread sackcloth and ashes under him?"

7. *Mita'am hamelech ug'dolav, By decree of the king and his great ones."* The King and his courtiers proclaim a fast which the people have already begun. They make official government policy that which began on a grassroots level.

V'habheima habakar v'hatzon, The beast, the cattle and the sheep." The animals fasting is another example of exaggeration in the book of Jonah.

8. *"V'yitcasu sakim haadam v'hab'heima, They shall be covered with sackcloth, man and beast."* Here is another step in exaggeration. Not only do these pious animals fast they also wear sackcloth.

"V'yashuvu ish midarco hara'ah, Let everyone turn back from his evil ways." The king understands that simply fasting, sitting in ashes covered in sackcloth will not be sufficient to receive forgiveness from God. His approach follows the prophecies of Isaiah. Above I quoted Isaiah denunciation of fasting, sackcloth, and ashes as the means to God's forgiveness. In 58:5–8, Isaiah goes on to say that God wants repentant people to turn to righteous living. "Then you shall call and the Eternal will answer" (Isa 58:9).

"Umin hachamas, And from the violence." This is the first time word *chamas* appears in the book of Jonah. The Hebrew Bible uses this term to describe the behavior of the generation of Noah whose evil behavior also triggers a proclamation of destruction from God in Genesis 6:13.

9. *"Mi yodei'ah, Who knows."* The king does not promise the Ninevites that these acts of repentance will save them. He does not begin this sentence "I know." Rather, he humbly tells his people that this might work.

10. *"Vayar Haelohim et ma'aseihem, The God saw their acts."* The <u>ha</u> stresses the point that this is <u>The One</u> God, not one of many gods. On the ship the sailors "cried out, each to his own god," seeking supernatural intervention to save them from the storm. Here, The One God acts to save the Ninevites.

The Ninevites did not merely declare faith in the Eternal. They turned from their evil paths in a way visible to God.

"Vayinachem Haelohim al hara'ah asher diber la'asot, And God repented of the evil He had planned to do." In Exodus 32:15 we find almost the identical phrase, describing God deciding not to destroy the Israelites following the incident of the Golden Calf. There the text reads, *"vayinachem YHVH al hara'ah asher diber la'asot, And the Eternal repented of the evil He had planned to do."* The only change is the substitution of *"Haelohim"* for "YHVH." We find the same phrase in Genesis 6:6 where in advance of the flood, we read of God's disappointment with the path humanity had taken. "YHVH repented that He had made man on earth."

Chapter Four

1. **"*Vayeira el-Yonah ra'ah gedola, It was evil to Jonah a great evil.*"** The verb, *"vayeira,"* and the noun, *"ra'ah,"* come from the same root referring to evil. Often the Hebrew Bible uses this device of a root appearing in both its verb and noun form in the same phrase. We understand this device to convey intense feeling or action. We can understand the repetition of this root to express the depths of Jonah's disappointment that God did not destroy Nineveh. We can translate the phrase "Jonah was deeply displeased."

The book of Nehemiah, 2:10, uses a similar phrase to describe the reaction of local Persian officials to the arrival of Nehemiah in the Land of Israel. *"Vayeira lahem ra'ah gedola, asher ba'adam l'vakeish tova livnei Yisrael*, It deeply displeased them that a man had come to seek the welfare of the children of Israel."* Our text replaces *"lahem"* with "Yonah."

2. **"*Vayitpaleil el-YHVH, And he prayed to the Eternal.*"** Throughout the Hebrew Bible this word introduces a petition to God for protection and salvation. In 4:2, the text uses this word conventionally, to introduce Jonah's petition to God for renewed life. Here Jonah, ironically, petitions God for death.

"*Halo zeh d'vari, Isn't this my word.*" The text of chapter one does not include Jonah reciting these words while he was still in his land.

"*Ki yadati, For I knew.*" Jonah, with colossal chutzpah, says, "I knew this was going to happen." How could he have known that the Ninevites would repent? The repentance of the Ninevites is an unprecedented act. This is a self-justifying declaration attempting to turn his fearful flight into an act motivated by a clear vision of the future.

"*El chanun v'rachum erech apayim v'rav chesed v'neecham al ha-raah, A compassionate and gracious God, slow to anger, abounding in kindness and renouncing evil.*" Jonah's description of God's forgiving nature from comes from Exodus 34:6. The Exodus passage continues on to praise God's kindness but also says that God does "not clear the guilty but visits the sins of the parents upon the children." Our author instead concludes the verse, *"v'nicham al hara'ah, And repenting of evil."* These final words come from *"vayinachem Haelohim al hara'ah,* and God repented of the evil."* (Jonah 3:10) Jonah uses this phrase from chapter three to express his disappointment that God has forgiven the Ninevites.

3. "***Kach na et nafsi mimeni, Take my soul from me.***" On board the ship Jonah was prepared to die to save the sailors. Now Jonah is apparently prepared to die because of wounded pride. He publicly predicted the destruction of Nineveh and God disappointed him by forgiving the repentant sinners. Jonah cannot bear the shame. We might have expected him to be proud of his accomplishment. He spoke and the Ninevites responded to him. Many of the prophets are ignored or even imprisoned. Jonah's success does not bring him joy. At the beginning of the story Jonah wants nothing to do with this mission to Nineveh because he thinks only of himself. Now with the mission successfully completed he again thinks only of himself.

In the belly of the fish, Jonah declares his compete devotion to God. When he first returns to dry land, he acts in loyal response to God's instruction and goes to Nineveh. But now that some time has passed, Jonah forgets those promises made in the belly of the fish. He returns to his self-centered view of the world.

Often people in trouble make deals with God. "If you save me, I will pray every day, I will come to the synagogue every week. I will turn my life around. I will . . ." When these people overcome their difficulty, they rarely keep up their end of the bargain over the long term.

4. "***Heiteiv chara-lecha, Are you goodly grieved?***" The first word of this phrase is connected to the familiar Hebrew word *tov*, good. Our text uses the root (Tet, Vav, Vet) in the Hipheel form. God speaks sarcastically to Jonah "Is it good for you to be so grieved?" Jonah's self-centered grief stuns God.

5. "***Vayeitzeu Yonah, And Jonah went out.***" The action described in this verse must have taken place right after Jonah made his declaration in 3:4. He waits to see what will happen to Nineveh. In Hebrew there is no separate past perfect form to describe action which had already been completed. Verbs in the regular past tense form are used for this purpose. So we can understand this verse to begin, "For Jonah had . . ." We saw a similar construction earlier in verse five of the first chapter.

6. "***Vay'man, Apportioned.***" This is the same word used to describe God's call of the big fish. A *manah* is a portion. Here we can take it to mean "provided." The same word appears in the next two sentences to describe God summoning the worm and the hot wind. God acts as a stage manager cueing the players, the fish, the plant, the worm and the wind when it is their moment to enter the action "on stage."

Mei'al Yonah, Over Jonah." In 4:2, Jonah quotes Exodus 34:6 to describe God as "slow to anger." Here God demonstrates great patience with Jonah. God does not simply dismiss Jonah's objection to the Divine acceptance of the Ninevites repentance. God uses the kikayon plant to teach Jonah to be concerned with the world beyond himself.

"Kikayon." No one knows what kind of plant this is. This is similar to the location of Tarshaish and the species of the big fish. None of these details are known and none of them are important. Tarshaish is some city outside the Land of Israel, the fish is some giant species big enough to swallow a person and the plant must be leafy enough to provide significant shade.

"Simcha gedolah, A great joy." Jonah is not simply happy about the plant, he is very happy. His great joy is another example of exaggeration. Also he does not thank God for the plant. Either he does not notice that the plant grew in a miraculous manner or he thinks it is just coming to him.

7. *"Lamacharat, To the next morning."* Overnight God removes the protection which had been provided the day before.

8. *"Ruach kadim charishit, A silencing east wind."* A hot wind which stifles all activity, well known to residents of the Middle East. In Israel today this wind is called by the Arabic word, *chamsin*. God does not only remove the kikayon plant, God literally turns up the heat. God places Jonah in great discomfort.

9. *"Heiteiv chara-lecha, Are you goodly grieved?"* Here and in the following verse the text uses this phrase from verse 4 to describe Jonah's sense of loss over the death of the plant. In this verse God asks the question sarcastically.

"Heiteiv chara-lee, I am goodly grieved." Jonah seem oblivious to God's sarcasm and uses this same phrase to describe his feelings.

10. *"Vayomeir YHVH, And the Eternal said."* God has to explain to Jonah the object lesson because Jonah cannot figure it out by himself.

11 *Asher lo yada bein y'mino lismolo, Who does not know his right from his left."* The text uses singular forms here to refer to each of the Ninevites. God explains to Jonah that the Ninevites deserve mercy because they are not an advanced society.

"Uvheima raba, Many beasts." God points out that the destruction of Nineveh would also have required the pointless slaughter of many animals.

The book of Jonah ends abruptly without telling us Jonah's response to God's lesson. Does Jonah learn? The sailors learned. They recognized the Eternal as the ruler of the universe. They made vows and sacrifices. The people of Nineveh learned. They repented for their sins and turned to God. Does Jonah learn? Is Jonah going to walk with God? By not answering this question the author allows us to place ourselves into the story at the end. The real question facing us as we conclude the book of Jonah is did we learn? Are we going to follow the examples of the sailors and the Ninevites by turning to God? Or will we remain self-absorbed like Jonah?